Corporate Cloak
& Dagger

£1·80

JAMES CROFT

CORPORATE CLOAK
& DAGGER

Inside the World
of Industrial Espionage

HarperCollins*Publishers*

HarperCollins*Publishers*
77–85 Fulham Palace Road
Hammersmith, London W6 8JB

A Paperback Original 1994
1 3 5 7 9 8 6 4 2

A catalogue record for this book
is available from the British Library

ISBN 0 00 638067 0

Set in Linotron Meridien by
Rowland Phototypesetting Limited
Bury St Edmunds, Suffolk

Printed in Great Britain by
HarperCollinsManufacturing Glasgow

This book is dedicated to the memory of my late father
who had many ideas but ran out of time

With the world in its present condition of extreme unrest and changing friendships and antagonisms and with our greatly reduced and weak military forces, it is more than ever vital to us to have good and timely information.

Winston Churchill
Letter to Lloyd George, 19 March 1920

If you know your enemy and yourself, you will win every battle. If you know yourself but not your enemy, for every battle won you will suffer a loss. But if you are ignorant of both your enemy and yourself you are a fool and certain to be defeated in every battle.

Sun Tzu
The Art of Battle

CONTENTS

ACKNOWLEDGEMENTS

The world of espionage has existed since time immemorial. It has required many people to make it a working reality. This book is no exception, and the author is grateful for the assistance provided by libraries, commercial database suppliers, Companies House, police sources, archives, journalistic sources and the various members of the special forces and intelligence community whose names cannot be mentioned for obvious reasons of security.

Special thanks must be reserved for Wilfred Henning of Robot Foto und Electronic Gmbh, Michael Pritchard, photographic historian, and to Christie's, South Kensington for permission to include their excellent photographs. Thanks should also be extended to Conrad Sandler of Spycatcher/Vasco, CCS, and to Jean-Paul da Costa for their assistance in providing and taking photographs respectively. David Lawrence of Classic Camera proved invaluable by introducing me to his camera collection.

Simon and Alison Wynn were long-suffering when I monopolized their computer in the early stages of writing, and Peter Chapman spent many an evening creating computer graphics for the diagrams. Roger Birtles and Patrick Harrison were wonderfully patient on matters of correspondence.

The Royal Geographical Society library produced valuable data on satellite photography, and I am especially grateful to Anne Hawkins of the EAGGF for her information on CAP remote sensing to counter EC fraud.

Finally, I should like to thank my wife, who understands motivation so well.

INTRODUCTION

A former law lecturer of mine once introduced the law of evidence to the assembled students by asking two questions, the one mathematical, the other historical. Amidst total silence in the lecture hall he wrote the following on the blackboard:

2 + 2 = ?
Charles I was beheaded on 30 January 1649 – True/False

He asked whether there was a mathematician or an historian in the house. No one answered. Two hapless individuals were chosen and the answers given were 4 and True respectively. When asked who agreed with them there were no volunteers. When asked to explain their method of reasoning, the answers given were that everyone knew that 2 + 2 had to equal 4 because mathematics is an exact science and 30 January 1649 was correct because no history book contradicted this statement. The students concerned were informed that while they might make perfectly adequate mathematicians or historians, they must modify their opinions if they were to succeed in the law. The correct answer was that there was no correct answer because both problems were dependent on further information being provided. Thus, in the first problem, the answer would depend on which mathematical base one was using – base 4 or base 10. While in the historical example, at the time of the execution of Charles I and the establishment of a republic in Great Britain there was a transition from the Julian calendar of Julius Caesar to the Gregorian calendar of Pope Gregory. This transition produced a sizeable margin of error. The answer should have been 'it depends' in each case.

This book has two purposes. First, in a defensive context, to

sound a warning to those who feel that they are secure from
prying eyes and ears. Second, taking the offensive, to show
how easy it can be to obtain information on the competition.
The kind of lateral thinking demonstrated above is the key to
intelligence-gathering. Those who lack the interest or ability
to question, define and analyse everything should proceed no
further with this study and should consider an alternative pur-
suit. For those with these inherent qualities of enquiry and
investigation, read on.

CHAPTER ONE

The Threat – A Brief History of Economic Espionage

> Espionage is needed by those who prepare for attack, for aggression
>
> Nikita Khrushchev, former Soviet President[1]

History is so littered with traitors and the consequences of their acts that no time has ever passed without reference being made to such people in religion, story-telling, art, music, literature, archaeology, and even the Bible.

In 1250 BC the Lord instructed Moses to send twelve secret agents 'to explore the land of Canaan', and gave him useful advice on selection criteria for espionage work. Thus in Numbers XIII the Lord insisted on the choice of 'leaders' from each of the twelve tribes of Israel for intelligence work. As a result, Moses told his agents to: 'Go north from here into the southern part of the land of Canaan and then on into the hill-country. Find out what kind of country it is, how many people live there, and how strong they are. Find out whether the land is good or bad and whether the people live in open towns or in fortified cities. Find out whether the soil is fertile and whether the land is wooded. And be sure to bring back some of the fruit that grows there.'[2] Regrettably their good intelligence was badly used and as a consequence the people of Israel spent forty years in the wilderness. Their eventual arrival in the Promised Land was preempted by an espionage operation that employed Rahab the harlot behind enemy lines and assisted in the defeat of Jericho by Joshua.[3] Jericho's fall was novel, but the actual intelligence operation preceding it was conventional.

Delilah was an infamous spy for the Philistines. Alfred the Great countered the Danish threat by assessing the enemy's strength disguised as a Bard and infiltrating the Danish camp in the process. Akbar, the Mogul of India, had several thousand agents reporting to him on a regular basis.[4] Even in Elizabethan times, Sir Francis Walsingham set up a privately funded secret service to protect Queen Elizabeth I's throne from the Jesuits and sent agents abroad to gather intelligence on the Spanish Armada.[5] Indeed, it was Sir Francis Walsingham who provided the evidence that led to the execution of Mary Queen of Scots. The establishment of the Republic of Oliver Cromwell in 1649 was no exception, and the Lord Protector ran agents via his secretary, John Thurloe. Little changed with the restoration of the monarchy in 1660. Charles II used the Reverend John Wallis, the Cambridge mathematician who decrypted Charles I's coded despatches for Parliament during the English Civil War. Across the Atlantic, Abraham Lincoln had to rely on the private sector to assist him when the American Civil War started – he employed Allan Pinkerton's detective agency to perform his intelligence work.[6]

As the world has become more competitive and complex, so has intelligence-gathering become more prolific. Corporate intelligence gathering is practised not only by those interested in risk analysis for potential mergers and acquisitions or takeover battles, but also by those seeking to outdo their business rivals by obtaining information on their strengths, weaknesses and products, by those interested in counterfeiting and illegal reproduction, and also by governments (particularly totalitarian ones) obsessed with the need to find out about their neighbours.

Historically, much industrial espionage has been state-sponsored. During World War II there was massive German interest in US industry because of the level of its industrial development, research and innovation, which was vitally important for a country undergoing a vast rearmament programme. Indeed, the German industrial concerns IG Farben and Krupp briefed their US representatives to report to their head office on military and industrial development. In his book *The Game of the Foxes*, Ladislas Farrago quoted an Abwehr officer of 1934: 'In every armament factory, in every shipyard in America, we have a spy, several of them in key positions. The United States cannot plan a warship, design an airplane, develop a new device, that we do not know at once.'[7]

An examination of German World War II files shows the wide range of material that the Abwehr agents obtained – blueprints for equipment such as aircraft landing gear, new ships and developmental aircraft; details of production capacity and expansion programmes; and timetables for a switch from a peacetime footing to all-out production.

Prior to World War II, US and German companies entered into a variety of cartel agreements providing for the free exchange of new inventions and licences to cover their manufacture. Thus Sperry Gyroscope licensed The Ascania Company to manufacture sound-indicators and blind-flying instruments in Germany and supplied the Germans with gyroscopes and other aircraft instruments. Pratt and Whitney provided the Germans with engines, propellers and spare parts including giving Bayerische Motoran Werke details of all research and development work in the United States. Standard Oil and IG Farben formed an agreement to exchange patents and research, and the Germans received the formula and process for making butyl rubber, a major strategic material, and, rather more ominously, a superior method for making explosives. Thomas H. Etzold has said that: 'In April 1934, the American commercial attaché in Berlin reported that American representatives were selling all kinds of aviation equipment – motor parts, crankshafts, cylinder heads, automatic pilots, gyro compasses and other instruments, and fine control systems for anti-aircraft guns, and not just in sample quantities but in volume.'[8] Thus by June 1940, of the twenty specialist items on the US Government's list of scarce and strategic materials vital to the nation's defence, fourteen were produced by companies that were in contact with German firms. In the words of Ladislas Farrago, without espionage 'the Germans could not have gone to war as soon as they did'.

However, this century has been dominated more by the USSR and the Communist obsession with stealing the West's state and industrial secrets. As far back as the 1930s, when two Soviet defectors to the West, General Alexander Orlov and Walter Krivitsky, tried in vain to warn of Soviet high-level penetration of Western societies,[9] the threat has been very real, and examples are to be found in Great Britain in 1964, when Soviet trade representative Vladimir I. Solomatin was caught trying to obtain samples of electrical equipment banned from export to the USSR,[10] to a range of other countries, including Argentina, Italy, France, Japan, Australia, Tunisia, Cyprus, Morocco, Spain, Denmark, Sweden, Norway and the USA.

It is a popular misconception that the KGB was interested only in national or governmental secrets related to defence. The KGB are very interested in economic matters, especially as their economy has always lagged far behind that of the West. Indeed, so important are economic matters to the KGB that Roger Hillsman of Columbia University has said that if the Kremlin were forced to choose between subverting the National Security Advisor to the President and a long-term subscription to the *New York Times*, it would select the *New York Times*, because the Russians prefer a wide range of information to narrow, if high-level, material.[11] Harry Rositzke has described the typical KGB officer of the 1980s as an erudite science or economics graduate busy at work in New York and Europe, 'developing friendly contacts with persons of influence across the spectrum of private and public élites: politicians of the Centre and Right as well as the Left, Labour leaders of all political complexions, key editors and journalists of all hues, and prominent members of the business and banking communities.'[12]

With the collapse of Communism in the Eastern bloc, a naive optimist might be led to believe that the threat of this prominent aspect of industrial espionage and corporate intelligence-gathering is over. They would be wrong. The vacuum left by the end of the Soviet empire must be filled. The move towards Western-style democracy and free-market enterprise will mean a rush to catch up with the West. This is dangerous though inevitable. Industrial espionage manifests itself in a variety of ways, many of which will now be explored in this book, but the key element is its hydra-headed quality. State-sponsored corporate intelligence-gathering may have been compromised, but classic corporate intelligence work will now make increased demands on our society, and with labour costs inevitably falling in the Eastern bloc, we ignore it at our peril. Now is not a time for complacency.

CHAPTER TWO

The Hunt for Knowledge –
Overt Intelligence-Gathering

Seek and ye shall find; knock and it shall be opened
unto you

St Matthew[1]

It is a tribute to a democratic society that large amounts of
information are freely available to the general public. Not only
can this render the exercise of intelligence-gathering more
cost-effective, but it will also make the investigator's job considerably easier.

LIBRARIES

Libraries are the first place to consider, as every major town
or city has them and many, through a scheme known as library
exchange, will have the capacity to link up with others to
obtain information not readily available at the local branch.

Within the UK, statute demands that certain libraries comply
with the UK Design, Copyright and Patent Act 1988 and have
copies of all material published. These comprise the British
Library, the Bodleian Library at Oxford University, Cambridge
University Library, the National Library of Wales in Aberystwyth, the National Library of Scotland in Edinburgh, and
Trinity College Library in Dublin. In addition, all copies of
copyrighted magazines and newspapers are kept at the British
Library at Colindale in North London. Each of these libraries

has vast resources available, but a 'fishing exercise' is often not very helpful as it is too time-consuming. One useful factor is that contents indices are kept on microfiche, and a complete list of titles of books, reports, magazines and periodicals can easily be obtained by entering key words relating to the subject matter (e.g. industrial espionage, business intelligence, fraud).

Many companies have their own libraries, and some groundwork can be done here. For more technical information relating to trades or professions, you could consider using specialized libraries which are normally restricted to members only; however, an element of guile together with a convincing cover-story (a classic one is that you are researching for your post-graduate doctoral thesis) and the offer of a fee is normally enough to grant one access.

SPECIALIST LIBRARIES

Some of the most useful libraries are those that specialize in a trade or profession. For example, each of the various libraries of the four Inns of Court, the libraries of the Institutes of Bankers, Chartered Accountants, Chartered Surveyors and Directors contain academic and practical works dealing specifically with the professions they represent. As much industrial espionage or pro-active market research will be concentrated on technical, scientific, business and commercial matters as well as patents, trade marks, designs and international standards, the Science Reference and Information Service in London should be consulted. Certain specialized university or polytechnic handbooks (e.g. UCCA/PCAS) can be consulted to identify subject matter; from there, contact their libraries or prominent lecturers who are generally more than happy to assist with advice.

REFERENCE LIBRARIES

Reference libraries are crucial sources of information. While most ordinary libraries contain a reference section, pure reference libraries are seldom found outside cities and larger towns. They house national and international telephone directories, professional directories ranging from personnel managers to the military, which are ideal for verifying qualifications on people's curriculum vitae, and often copies of *Kompass* and *Standard and Poor* directories, which contain basic information on some UK and US registered companies.

Probably the best reference library in the country is the City Business Library on London Wall. This houses an impressive international economic section organized country by country, and is an excellent starting point for any form of corporate intelligence-gathering exercise. Of particular interest are the economic analyses of the larger private and state-owned companies. As an aide-memoire, the two main guides to reference materials in the UK are the *Aslib Directory of Information Sources in the UK* and *Croner's A–Z of Business Information Systems*.

TRADE OR PROFESSIONAL DIRECTORIES

Trades and professions have created standards of conduct and codes of behaviour that must be acknowledged and adhered to so as to protect the good name of these professional bodies and their members. As a result, qualifications can quite easily be checked by a simple phone call to the body in question. This may be far more cost-effective than visiting libraries. A list of the more popular institutions can be found in Appendix 2.

CORPORATE INTELLIGENCE SOURCES

Although Chapter 5 deals with this subject more fully, it its worth pointing out here that one of the best sources of information for UK registered companies is Companies House in London. In Europe, company details are filed at the Chamber of Commerce local to the company concerned, while in the USA, the Securities and Exchange Commission (SEC) requires public limited companies (PLCs) to submit details on an annual (10K) and a quarterly form (10Q). Commercial mortgages are dealt with by the Uniform Commercial Codes (UCC).

All UK registered companies file for the purpose of being classified as limited liability companies. One of the consequences of this is that they have a duty to make full and frank public disclosure of various documents, and these details may be consulted on microfiche at Companies House. The type of information that can be obtained includes:

1 Profit and loss accounts
2 Balance sheets
3 Source and application of funds statements
4 Registered office
5 Directors' reports
6 Register of members
7 Details of directors, company secretary and occasionally dates of birth and addresses
8 Directors' interests in shares and details of other share holders
9 Register of debenture holders
10 Mortgages and charges

All this information can be used as a basis for financial analysis to provide a range of corporate intelligence information, including overall profitability and long-term prospects.

In addition to the manual method of retrieving information at Companies House, an alternative, quicker but more costly method is to arrange for an on-line commercial database link-up with one of the numerous on-line services available in the market-place. For example, individual and company information services are available through CCN and Infolink, which will provide a company's most recent accounts, details of current directors and shareholders, bankers, accountants, the company's registered office, and also details of mortgages and any adverse factors affecting the company such as impending dissolution, loans, or problems with the civil courts. In addition, some of the available services provide accounting ratios for each company. Much of the information can be retrieved in minutes using an appropriate modem link.

For both UK and international service, it is possible to subscribe to Dun and Bradstreet, Jordan's, and M. W. Douglas, who offer an overall appraisal of a company's performance and use accounting ratios to assess performance. They will also sometimes consult bankers, financial advisers and accountants, but the disadvantage is that much of the information will be furnished by the company itself and its impartiality must therefore be questioned. Access to the system is normally by means of a personalized code; payment is by annual subscription and ad hoc charges dependent on the level of use.

STATISTICAL ANALYSIS

This can be invaluable for evaluating potential mergers and acquisitions, takeovers and competitor intelligence. Obvious UK-based sources of statistical information include reference libraries and specialized publications on companies and industries from the following sources: the *Financial Times*, *The Times*, *The Economist*, Library of the Office of Fair Trading, Library of the Monopolies and Mergers Commission, Library of the Ministry of Defence, Library of the Department of Trade and Industry (for the statistics and market intelligence of the British Overseas Trade Board), and the libraries of the institutes of various professional bodies. Additional statistical information can be obtained from Extel – a subscription system that provides both hard copy and on-line database access to all PLCs and various Unlisted Securities Market (USM) companies. Extel cards are available in most City law and accountancy firms, as well as in banks and the offices of up-market newspapers.

OFFSHORE COMPANIES

The ease with which international business is now conducted and the sheer internationalism of many business transactions mean that the popularity of offshore companies has increased rapidly. They first rose to prominence as part of elaborate tax-avoidance schemes under successive Labour governments. Many well-known companies take advantage of these schemes. However, offshore companies are also favoured because of the very limited amount of information it is necessary to disclose and the practice of using nominee directors and share holdings. These discreet and 'no questions asked' schemes have become so widespread that many companies advertise in both the daily and Sunday newspapers for a specialized offshore service in areas including Vanuatu, the British Virgin Islands, Liberia, Panama and the Channel Islands. A specific chapter will highlight the advantages of using an offshore company as a vehicle for anonymity later in this book.

ELECTRONIC LIBRARIES

On-line databases have already been mentioned. It is now possible to use them not only in specialist subject areas but also to gain access to all general newspaper articles from a set past date when input was started to the present.

The advent of these database systems has completely revolutionized corporate intelligence-gathering as, depending on the speed of the available modem and printer, one can have within seconds all available details on a set subject, an individual, a product of a company or institution – and all with the tap of a few computer keys. The systems are varied and are being modified all the time. The original systems were not intended as commercial vehicles but rather as a means of propagating ideas within academic circles; nowadays, however, some systems are being used solely for commercial purposes. The information net has spread, and for an agreed fee one can now access a chosen system at any point.

The success of these systems and their rapid penetration has been a feature of the computer and information technology (IT) generation. Traditional printing practices of copperplate print have been superseded by computer-console-fed fingertip data. Revolutions in international financial markets have meant that more and more information is needed both currently and historically to determine policy and thus profit. In addition, the massive expansion of the personal computer market and the reduction in the costs of hardware and software have contributed to this massive growth in consumer demand. As a result, the amount of information available internationally and historically is vast.

Within the electronic information industry there exist three classes – originators, hosts and consumers. The originators are the publishers or database producers. Often such people will deal with a host who will then deal with the consumer directly. Occasionally the host and the originator will be the same institution. A parallel can therefore be drawn with a typical business flow chart:

SUPPLIER → WHOLESALER → RETAILER → CUSTOMER
ORIGINATOR → HOST → CONSUMER

The host will possess a large mainframe computer system with a software capacity to select, group and translate a mass of raw data into a consumer package. Typical hosts in the USA and UK are BRS, FT Profile, Lexis/Nexis, Dialog and Pergamon Financial Data Services. A consumer will normally pay an introductory fee and an annual or monthly subscription, even when the system is not being used, possibly undergo a training course, and then pay an ad hoc charge for user time and the volume of print generated on a line-charged basis. Certain databases operate their own idiosyncratic systems, such as connect-time charges, or discounts for logging on in anti-social hours, and these idiosyncrasies are often voiced in each host firm's marketing material. The benefits can be enormous and are ideal for any firm seriously considering focusing resources on corporate intelligence-gathering, but for a small firm with minimal use then the costs could prove a major deterrent. A list of recommended firms offering on-line services can be found in Appendix 3.

Computers are simple tools, even though the middle-aged and the uninitiated may believe that they lack the capacity or the will to learn how systems operate. The success of the computer has mainly been due to consumer-led demand rather than to the scientific kudos of developing more sophisticated systems than the competition. Indeed, this success would not have been possible if systems had not been targeted at the mass market. While more advanced systems, such as Fortran, can be left to the scientists, basic log-on procedure and command language are as easy as initiating a simple conversation in one's native tongue – in fact arguably more so, as the commands used are abbreviated ones and ignore such human characteristics of speech as tone, inflection, accent, simile and metaphor.

For example, the FT Profile system uses the following command structure:

SELECT	From a prescribed list of available sources, either individually or via 'group bookings' such as UK News or US News, which will provide the consumer with a broad range of daily and Sunday newspapers.
GET	Use a name of an individual, a product, a company or even a subject.
PICK	An additional, more specific command should the GET command not be specific enough.
HEADLINE	A brief summary of all available headlines of all articles.
CONTEXT	An abstract to give the theme of the article but not the full text.
TEXT	The article with full narrative, dialogue and punctuation.

In addition, with the PFDS system owned by the Pergamon Group, the 'X-FILE' command allows one to search all files at the same time, while 'DIALOG FINBUS' searches several separate databases simultaneously.

These commands will normally generate the required information, assuming that the database has the information and you have chosen your sources correctly. To be more selective, you should use the aforementioned command 'HEADLINE'. This will provide the dates and sources of all the articles and a brief heading. In this way you can eliminate the chaff and concentrate on the key areas, thus saving both time and money. Once this manual selection has taken place, you can be still more selective by choosing 'CONTEXT' to see if the article in question is really the one required. If so, then use the command 'TEXT'. Another important command available on some systems is 'MORE', whereby as one year's database is exhausted you request 'more' from the computer for each year until the entire memory has been exhausted. An additional point to remember is to use the command 'PRINT' to download information onto either disk or paper, as to transcribe material from the screen will take too long and cost too much.

In determining what you need in terms of equipment for these systems, the key criterion is genuine need. They are expensive, and you should ascertain that you have read all available background material to ensure that:

(a) You need the service yourself, as it may be cheaper to sub-contract and use professional researchers or intermediaries. Of these the largest in the UK is the FT Business Research Centre.

(b) You have the right service for your needs.

If the above criteria can be satisfied, then you should invest in the following hardware:

1 Personal computer, preferably with both hard and floppy disk-drive capacity.
2 Modem, which is the electronic device linking your computer to the telephone line – minimum 1200 baud (bits of data per second).
3 Printer. However, this is not absolutely necessary if one only needs to save the material electronically and not on hard copy.
4 CD-ROM system. These are used by some database originators and hosts. The advantage is the low cost of disk media, their durability and easy transferability. Some people have a preference for optical disks.

Apart from service charges, annual or monthly subscriptions, and the amortized costs of computer equipment (try a lease-hire arrangement), you also need to consider the lost

---

Advantages and Disadvantages of Electronic Databases

Advantages	Disadvantages
Fast	Expensive
Discreet	Risk of being vague
Cheap if controlled	Cursory information
Current/historic	Hearsay
National/international	No standard search
Picks others' brains first	
The 'edge' factor	

---

opportunity costs of your own user time. Having a fast modem and printer (2400 baud and advanced laser jet respectively) is advisable, as you will avoid wasting time while your system connects to the host/producer and prints the material. In addition, choose your modem carefully, as some will only work on the more advanced tone-generated systems, while much of BT's network remains on the old pulse-generated system.

Electronic databases can be used for a variety of different purposes, such as investigating:

1 The existence of an individual.
2 Loans, county court judgements, bankruptcy pertaining to individuals.
3 Company directorships.
4 Age.
5 Newsworthiness/notoriety/positive v. negative data.
6 Corporate records/statutory returns.
7 Holding companies and associated companies.
8 Share holdings – names and addresses.
9 Accounting ratios.
10 Credit ratings.

11 Market research reports.

12 Trade magazines and write-ups.

13 Profiles – individual/industrial/company.

14 Advertisements.

15 New products.

16 Past strategy – recent moves by employees, poaching and head-hunting.

17 Patents/trademarks/copyright details.

18 Clues to chain of events.

19 Assets – yachts, cars, property, art, etc.

20 Accountants.

21 Bankers.

22 Mortgages with dates and details of lender.

Thus, by employing these database systems sensibly and cost-effectively, one can automatically build up a basic intelligence profile on institutions, products, corporations and individuals.

THE GENERAL REGISTER OF BIRTHS, DEATHS AND MARRIAGES

Under the Births and Deaths Registration Act (1926), it is mandatory to register all births, deaths and marriages in the UK General Register at St Catherine's House in London.

The UK is unusual in this regard, as many countries either do not have a centralized system (France is regionalized down to town hall level) or, if they do, apply a similar central registration system to our own but either sheer incompetence (as in the Third World) or paranoia regarding security (as in Israel) makes consulting them very difficult unless done illegally via an intermediary for an appropriate fee. The register lists all births, deaths and marriages in the UK and has done so since 1836, although parochial registration of weddings, christenings and burials was initially introduced during the reign of Henry VIII in 1538. In addition, the register contains lists of these items in the context of military and consular matters.

The General Register is a useful source of information, as people will often lie about their ages or their names for a whole host of reasons. One of the more glamorous reasons was detailed in Frederick Forsyth's novel *The Day of the Jackal*,[2] in which the objective was to take on a new, untraceable identity. To achieve this the assassin searched in a graveyard for the name of a child who had died very young. With the child's age established from the gravestone, the next step was to obtain the original birth certificate from St Catherine's House. This was then used to obtain a passport in the name of the deceased child who, had he lived, would have been about the same age as the assassin. At this time there was no way of matching death certificates with birth certificates. This loophole has now been closed. Other reasons for seeking a change of identity might be vanity, a criminal past, or disreputable, though not necessarily criminal, conduct in school, university or the earlier stages of one's career. It may simply be motivated by social pretension because of a contrived name or a redundant social title.

A UK birth certificate will contain the following information:

1 Subject's full name
2 Mother's maiden and first names
3 Father's full name
4 Father's occupation
5 Address of family at time of birth
6 Gender of subject
7 Precise date of birth
8 Hospital or place of birth

A UK marriage certificate will contain the following information:

1 Full names of spouses
2 Full names of spouses' fathers
3 Occupation of spouses' fathers
4 Date of marriage

5 Area in which marriage takes place
6 Occupation of spouses
7 Addresses of spouses
8 Names of witnesses to the marriage
9 Ages of spouses – useful for then checking with the register of births

A UK death certificate will contain the following information:

1 Name of deceased
2 Address where death occurred
3 Name of person registering death
4 Date of death
5 Address of person registering death
6 Details of place where death registered
7 Relationship of person registering death to the deceased

While it is illegal to obtain positive or adverse data regarding an individual's criminal past, or lack of one, such enquiries are sometimes made either by befriending a helpful policeman or by employing a sub-contractor to do the job. To be absolutely certain of identity the subject's details should include full name and address, date of birth, height, name of father, and occupation of father – all of which they obtain from the birth certificate. A birth, death or marriage certificate costs £5.50 or £20, depending on whether they want the details within twelve or thirty-six hours.

Fortunately, security at St Catherine's House has recently been tightened up, and generally a request for a certificate will fail unless a significant amount about the person concerned is already known, such as the precise date and place of birth and the full names not only of the subject but also of the subject's parents. When engaged in corporate intelligence-gathering these details will seldom be known. To avoid this pitfall, investigators will arrange an interview with a senior member of staff at St Catherine's House and use a plausible pretext such as investigation of an insurance claim, a course of action which often secures assistance.

RELIGIOUS ORGANIZATIONS

Extremism is not confined to nationalism and politics. It can manifest itself in a far more personal and indefinable area – religion. One of the common failings but enduring qualities of the human spirit is trust, which often manifests itself too often too late. Certain radical religious groups make use of these factors and often target the children of wealthy individuals or indeed those individuals themselves – some of whom could be employees.

The Moonies and the Scientologists are among the better-known religious groups. The Scientologists are renowned for their system of diagnostics, a concept pioneered by the Scientologists' mentor and former leader L. Ron Hubbard. A classic method of recruitment, it is claimed, is to provide clean-cut over-achievers with a test in which they will automatically perform badly. The solution is of course to embark on a residential course of Scientology which is when many people become convinced by the principles of the movement.

Other extremist religious sects are renowned for allegedly luring wealthy children with trust-funds. A low-protein diet is apparently a popular method of reducing resistance to their ideology.

Even within the more established and respectable religions there are members with uncompromising attitudes – for example, in the Opus Dei movement within the Roman Catholic Church.

However, there are intelligence-gathering bodies set up to counter extremist groups – all very discreet but quite real. Should you have concerns about an employee directly or indirectly through his family, then you would be well advised to seek advice from these bodies, if only to learn just what you might be up against.

LOCAL CHURCH RECORDS

These can be an invaluable source of information in putting together a picture of family life in regional areas, as the local parish will normally have details of baptisms, marriages, deaths and confirmations within the local area. Their usefulness has been compromised since the 1960s with increased communications links and a rapid growth in geographic mobility caused by work and social aspirations. Even so, this affects only certain sectors of the population and this source can still be useful in genealogical intelligence-gathering.

Some of the main problems involved are the cost of travelling to local areas and the fact that churches are often closed, church wardens away, and the files in a chaotic state. A fast and cost-effective method of circumventing these problems is to visit the UK headquarters of the Utah-based Mormon Church in Kensington, London. As part of their global quest to rebaptize the world, both living and dead, the Mormons send out their missionaries to record and note all available data on individuals living and dead that is recorded in local church records. These details are stored in microfilmed records in air-conditioned caves deep within the mountains that surround Salt Lake City in Utah. The service is fast, friendly, free of charge, and there is no pressure to join the Mormon Church. Such a system can also be of great assistance to lawyers who are seeking claimants in matters of probate.

BOGUS OR QUESTIONABLE TITLES

It was Noel Coward who coined the phrase 'The stately homes of England, how beautiful they stand, to prove the upper classes, have still the upper hand'[3], and there is no doubt that many confidence tricksters feel more confident using titles to pursue their business.

The move towards Soviet-inspired totalitarianism in Eastern Europe created a mass migration westwards, some of the people involved having perfectly legitimate claims to titles. Within the older Western European republics there are still people with legitimate titles. However, an increasingly popular practice has been for individuals to 'acquire' redundant or non-existent titles from areas of the world where it is very hard to trace their true origin. An additional problem is that the rules of primogeniture in the UK, whereby the hereditary title will pass only to the first-born son, and if there are only daughters as issue then it will lapse, are radically different from other countries in Europe where the title passes regardless of age, gender or order of birth.

While *Debrett* and the now redundant *Burke's Peerage* provide ample details of individuals with titles in the UK, the nearest that one gets to European nobility is the Marquis of Ruvigny's *Titled Nobility of Europe*, which was published only once, in 1913. The timing was unfortunate, with many entrants either being killed or displaced by the consequences of World War I. As a result, the chances of impostors appearing are legion. Fortunately, fewer and fewer people are impressed by purely social leanings, and it is professional qualifications and the lack of a civil or criminal record that really count in the modern world.

THE LAND REGISTRY

The Land Registry is a Civil Service executive agency responsible for the registration of title to land in England and Wales. Not all land in England and Wales is yet registered, but the Land Registry has information about 13.25 million of the estimated twenty-two million property titles in England and Wales. The Registry has index maps available for public inspection that indicate which properties are registered and which are not. The main reasons for land being unregistered is that it is subject to a lease of less than twenty-five years or is an old country property automatically passed down from one generation to another.

A search of the Land Registry requires the use of a variety of forms, depending on what information is required. The Registry is particularly useful when attempting to identify assets and determine where a person has put his money, which may have been stolen from an employer, or ascertain whether the land is subject to a mortgage, which could determine whether or not it is worth suing the subject.

Each individual register is identified by a title number that is unique to the property it describes, and each register is divided into three parts – the *property register*, the *proprietorship register*, and the *charges register*. In addition, the extent of the registered land is shown on the associated title plan, and occasionally specific documents referred to in the register are on file. The Registry will have all details relating to a set piece of registered land. For example, the *property register* will identify the geographical location and the extent of the registered property by using a short narrative description. This register will also occasionally provide details of any rights that benefit the land, such as a right of way over adjoining land. For leasehold titles brief details of the lease itself are given. The official title plan is based on large-scale Ordnance Survey maps.

The *proprietorship register* describes the quality of the title, which will normally be an absolute title where the Registry is satisfied as to the property's true ownership. The name and address of the legal owner will also be provided and the register will also detail any restrictive covenants on the owner's power to sell, mortgage or otherwise deal with the land. Often proprietorship will be vested in the name of a company or a trust, and here again the parameters of alternative intelligence-gathering should be explored.

The *charges register* includes key particulars of registered mortgages, and also provides the investigator with notice of other financial burdens secured on the property and details of other rights and interests to which the property is subject, such as leases, rights of way or restrictive covenants.

There are three methods of inspection available to an

enquirer corresponding to three different Land Registry forms, namely:

1 Form 109. This is the best and the most convenient method of obtaining information from the Registry. It can be used by post or by fax, one Form 109 being required for each registered title requested. Ideally one should know the title number, but it is possible to leave this part blank and pay an additional small charge of £7 to get the Land Registry to check the Public Index for you. The total charge in 1992 for this service, including a map of the property, was £21.

2 Form 110. This is used to inspect copies of documents referred to on the register. A charge of £7 is made, but it should be noted that the rules on public inspection are not as thorough as for Form 109, and that copies of leases or charges referred to on the register of titles are not generally open to public inspection.

3 Form 111. This is used when one needs to make a personal inspection of the register by visiting the appropriate district Land Registry. In 1992 the charge for this service was £21. The option will only be useful to the investigator if he is in the vicinity of the local Land Registry, otherwise the exercise will be both time-consuming and costly.

While it is possible to seek information without knowing the registered title number, any request for the Land Registry to supply details when the land concerned is in the countryside is likely to be returned with a request for the title number to be provided, as well as a detailed map showing the demarcation lines of the land in question. To pay a visit to the area is generally not cost-effective, and there is a risk that the target will be alerted, especially if that person is a competitor or an existing employee.

To solve this problem it is wise to visit either the London Map Centre in Victoria, the Map Room of the Royal Geographic Society, or Stanford's map shop in Covent Garden and ask for detailed 1:12,500 or 1:2500 maps of the area in question. The RGS is open to Fellows only; at Stanford's the cost of a specialist map is £20, but the result is generally good enough to satisfy the Land Registry. Stanford's have full maps of London and the South-East permanently in stock. To order from other areas of the country, there is a time-lapse factor of approximately four days.

The following information is not available from the Land Registry:

(a) Individual tenancy agreements.
(b) Details of planning permission, compulsory purchase, land redevelopment, road charges, public health charges, building lines or tree conservation. These matters are recorded as local land charges by the local authority.
(c) Unregistered titles.
(d) Land or property values.
(e) Land held under a lease for a term of twenty-one years or less.
(f) Land outside of England and Wales.
(g) Matters concerning the community charge or council tax.

These limitations can be overcome by using alternative sources of overt intelligence-gathering, such as local authority records and the voters roll.

THE VOTERS ROLL

Under the Representation of the People Act (1983) every person in the UK is entitled to vote in national and local elections unless they are excluded by youth (under eighteen years of age), a criminal record (and are not covered by the Rehabilitation of Offenders Act (1974)), by reason of insanity, or because they are from overseas. These details are a matter for the public record, although it is possible to avoid your name being made public if your career or position make you a security risk.

For those who have electronic link-ups with consumer credit database checklists such as CCN or Infolink, these systems use the voters roll as the first port of call. Such on-line systems will also give the names of others listed at that address and, in the case of recent additions such as children, the year in which they reached the age of majority (eighteen). In turn, this can lead to information on the parents by obtaining the birth certificates of the children in the manner already described.

THE COMMUNITY CHARGE REGISTER

While this has now been replaced by the council tax, there will still be records of community charge-payers at council level. The community charge is often referred to as the 'poll tax', as local authorities use the voters roll lists as guidance for identifying inhabitants of their boroughs. In addition, each form will be sent to 'the occupier' of a certain address where no name is listed on the voters roll, and failure to register could result in legal action being taken. An additional bonus of the community charge register is that it represents a public record, and only security concerns will keep one's name off it. To be especially safe some people register using a different name and ensure that all their bills are paid promptly in cash. A useful plus in the field of corporate intelligence-gathering is that more and more people are being encouraged to pay their bills automatically by standing order or direct debit, and with imaginative and discreet methods it is normally possible to obtain a person's bank account details.

PLANNING DEPARTMENTS

All local authorities have planning departments, and any desire to construct, adapt or build any new or existing structure must satisfy the whims and fancies of the local planning officer.

Different areas have different criteria, but the one that is uniform is the formal procedure needed to planned development authorized. The old maxim Englishman's home is his castle' has been severely compromised of late. Indeed, it is standard practice to display the proposed alterations in a public place and invite members of the public to voice their objections to the scheme. If you are troubled by even a hint of employee dishonesty and have evidence that the employee concerned has been spending lavishly on roof conversions or new wings, then it is advisable to seek details of the property in question from the local planning department. For a small fee they will provide you with details of the planning request, but not the architect's drawings which remain the private property of the architect.

ESTATE AGENTS

Estate agents represent a good local source of property and land values for rural and built-up areas. All enquiries can be made as soon as you have identified a property or land via the Land Registry. Often the estate agent will have been brought up in the locality and will have extensive knowledge of the area's price fluctuations.

THE LAW COURTS

A visit to the Law Courts on the Strand in London can provide one with information on any legal action concerning an individual or a company as either plaintiff or defendant, including writs and petitions issued, pending cases, actual judgements, bankruptcy and divorces. The same information can occasionally be found in newspapers or trade magazines, though often in an abbreviated format. The larger on-line credit electronic database services such as CCN and Infolink contain details of outstanding county court judgements.

TRADE EXHIBITIONS

Almost every trade, profession or industry holds a trade exhibition once or twice a year in various exhibition halls around the world. In London, Olympia, Earls Court and the Islington Business Centre are popular venues. At these exhibitions one finds a plethora of different firms all vying with one another to show that their product is better than next door's. The opportunities for free intelligence-gathering in the form of public relations and product hand-outs followed by client contact are excellent. Examples of trade exhibitions for the security industry are Copex at Sandown racetrack in Surrey, and Ifsec, which is held in Olympia in the spring. Often the free trade or PR magazines are springboards to further information. It is commonly accepted that a great deal of industrial espionage takes place at such events, not only by business competitors but also by overseas governments.

TRADE NEWS

A wise investment is *Willings Press Guide*, which gives details of over seven thousand UK magazines, newspapers and journals that service a host of professions and industries in the United Kingdom. The latest personnel, key figures, mergers and acquisitions, and product information will be detailed, and occasionally interviews given that provide a guide to market confidence. Items of trade news will also cover advertising and job applications. An example of trade press within the security industry is *Professional Security*, which is given away to all members of the International Professional Security Association. Sometimes the only way one can receive trade news is by belonging to one of the trades or professions, which often involves taking onerous examinations. In such cases, consult a library or use the pretext of doing research to gain access. No trade or profession likes to have bad public relations.

NEWSPAPER CUTTINGS

We have already talked about the subject of electronic access to newspapers and magazines. The cost and practicality of these systems can be a hindrance. An alternative, cost-effective method is to contact one of the United Kingdom newspaper cuttings services, such as Newsclip, CXT, Romeike and Currice, Durrant's and Standard Press Cuttings, and use their services on a purely contractual basis. While there will be a monthly charge, it is not prohibitive, and the actual cuttings charges are a lot cheaper than their electronic equivalent. Information is sent by post, fax or courier. Many companies now use their libraries to perform an in-house service to be sure of what the market is saying about both their competitors and themselves.

'FREEBIES'

Much information can be obtained in this way with no pretext needed. In other cases you may need some sort of cover-story. Although some trade magazines require a subscription, others are obtainable free of charge. Other 'freebies' are public relations hand-outs, trade catalogues, company and stockbrokers' reports. It is always a good idea to have a 'dump' mailing address for correspondence.

Among the aforementioned list of 'freebies', stockbrokers' reports have become key economic indicators, and their leading employees have achieved the status of economic gurus. Barely a day passes without X individual from Y company being interviewed on television or radio. Many are part of the London-based Society of Investment Analysts which has over 2500 members. Some of their information will be passed to you with the minimum of pretext, but a better method is to befriend someone 'inside' the organization, flatter them, and suggest that you can offer information in exchange. This method is popular with financial journalists. A list of prominent investment houses providing these economic indicators can be found in Appendix 4.

THE ROLE OF THE MARKET RESEARCHER

Market researchers are to be found in libraries and the press, but there are also companies with tentacles that transcend national boundaries. There are about fifteen such companies based in the United Kingdom that specialize in the regular publishing of industry-specific information, and also in general corporate and industrial data. The largest firm in the world offering market research is Dun and Bradstreet, which has offices in forty countries and an annual turnover of $1.26 billion. Another similar firm is Jordan's. One of the limitations of these firms is that they are 'fed' information voluntarily by the target company concerned, and their information may be out of date and not always objectively researched. However, they have definite uses. They apply an automatic classification to each company to assess its credit rating – a good first step in corporate intelligence-gathering.

PATENTS OFFICE

A preliminary enquiry should always be made at the patent office in any country as this will save a great deal of time in other investigations. The UK Patents Office is open to the public and the service is free. The heaviest users tend to be companies seeking information about their competitors. A detailed discussion of the workings of the UK Patents Office can be found in Chapter 6.

GOVERNMENT STATISTI

Most governments publish vast amounts of offic
and other data on a variety of issues including the
professions. The cost is not normally prohibitive. ... ... UK,
the official government publisher is Her Majesty's Stationery
Office (HMSO), while in the USA it is the Government Printing
Office (GPO). Lists of contents are readily available and the
service is generally fast.

TELEPHONE LISTS

This is a cost-effective way of establishing whether a person
lives at a particular address and can be of use historically as
well by checking on earlier directories in library archives.
International telephone directories are available in the better-
equipped UK libraries and in most embassy libraries. BT
now offers electronic Yellow Pages for classified business
information and in 1990 launched its complete directory
on-line – Phonebase. It also provides its electronic directories
in microfiche and CD-ROM formats.

KELLY'S BUSINESS DIRECTORY

Available either electronically or in book format, the directory
lists over eighty thousand UK companies with basic details
under numerous headings. It includes maps of the area within
the M25 and details company locations street by street. The
directory is updated annually. Most reference libraries will
have copies.

VEHICLE REGISTRATION RECORDS

While this information is available to the public in many Western countries, this is not the case in the UK where the information is held by the Driver and Vehicle Licensing Centre (DVLC) in Swansea. Unless you consider using subterfuge, or were the victim of an incident involving the vehicle in question, there is at present no way of accessing this information legally, unless you employ a Hire Purchase Index (HPI) check on the vehicle registration number.

HPI's database was established in 1938 to help finance houses counter fraud in the motor industry. There are now in excess of seventeen thousand subscribers to HPI and the database currently holds ninety million references. An HPI Autodata helpline can be contacted on 0722 422422; this is open to the public, and for a small fee you will be able to find out the name of the financing or leasing company involved and the details of the transaction. Armed with this information, you can then contact the finance company direct. Quote the details already known, and ask for the settlement figure and confirmatory details of the name and address of the person who entered into the hire-purchase agreement. These details will generally be given automatically.

PUBLIC RECORD OFFICE

Split between offices in London's Chancery Lane and Kew in south-west London, the PRO houses collections of data ranging from selective intelligence reports to local town hall statistics, including details of the voluntary registration of people's changes of name. A complete list of publicly available information can be found either on microfiche or hard copy at both branches of the PRO.

CHAPTER THREE

The Hunt for Knowledge –
Covert Intelligence-Gathering

The truth is rarely pure and never simple
Oscar Wilde[1]

This chapter will concentrate on intelligence-gathering by covert methods. For most enterprises, the acquisition of knowledge by the overt methods described in Chapter 2 will more than satisfy the objective. However, intense pressure, the need to avoid leaving 'footprints' in any of the sources detailed in the previous chapter, or paranoia may lead one to seek more desperate remedies. Some, but not all, of these methods are illegal.

RUBBISH CHECKS

The collection and analysis of commercial and domestic rubbish is a well-practised method of data collection. Even the fictional detective Sherlock Holmes employed the method in 'The Hound of the Baskervilles' when he gave one of his 'Street Arabs' one shilling to bribe the outside porter in each of the twenty-three hotels in the Charing Cross area in order to 'see the waste paper of yesterday. You will say that an important telegram had miscarried, and that you are looking for it.'[2]

As intelligence agencies and private investigation companies use this method as a means of putting together financial or political profiles, they tend to give a sleazy image to the

practices of market researchers and social scientists who analyse the data for less sinister reasons. The study of rubbish has
actually reached the campuses of certain American universities. The University of Arizona offers a programme entitled
'Modern Material Studies'. These practices appear to be far
more popular in the USA than in the UK. The former field
director of Harvard University, Fred Gorman, has said of the
tactic: 'We can learn a great deal about people's domestic con-
sumption habits that span not only the range of foods consumed, but also medicines, potentially addictive substances,
alcohol, tobacco, and other types of narcotics. It's possible to
gain information even of a financial nature.'[3] Certainly, some
major US companies have recently been engaged in court dis-
putes regarding allegations of 'dumpster raiding'.[4]

Practitioners may occasionally include investigative journalists. Indeed, two *Sunday Times Magazine* journalists, Bruno
Mouran and Pascal Rostain, once set out to obtain details of
'the flashiest trash in Los Angeles'[5], which included that of
Jack Nicholson, Madonna and Ronald Reagan.

What to look for?

1 *Domestic rubbish*
  (a) Evidence of expenditure
  (b) Invoices/bills
  (c) Bank statements
  (d) Credit card statements or slips
  (e) Drugs
  (f) Drink – quantity and type
  (g) Medicine wrappers
  (h) Correspondence
  (i) Discarded work taken home
  (j) Discarded faxes or computer print-outs
  (k) Evidence of family problems

Where there is concern about an employee's mental stability, his absenteeism or possible dishonesty, this procedure can be of enormous use. In addition, when a potential takeover is being considered, some consider it a good idea to target not just the company, its lawyers, accountants and public relations people, but also the private homes of its principal officers.

2 Office rubbish
(a) Memos/reports
(b) Computer material
(c) Fax sheets containing fax numbers and name of sender
(d) Internal telephone directories
(e) Computer manuals
(f) Credit card counterfoils
(g) Bank details
(h) Abandoned floppy disks
(i) Abandoned typewriter carbons
(j) Invoices and delivery notes of raw materials
(k) Client lists

3 Factory-floor rubbish
(a) Throw-away cuts
(b) Cartons, produce containers and boxes which can give an indication of contents, ingredients and volume
(c) Industrial waste and by-products which are of particular use to environmental groups and, as with all intelligence-gathering, need not be limited to situations where pollution is suspected

Of major concern to all persons who engage in this form of intelligence-gathering is the question of legality. The recent BA/Virgin Atlantic industrial espionage case has pushed this issue to the forefront of journalistic comment, and the case will be discussed later. The British Airways escapade was not an isolated incident. The *Sunday Times* reported in November 1991 that Williams Holdings PLC believed itself to be the victim of a dirty tricks war after private investigators, employed by a bank helping to defend an electronics firm from Williams' £700 million takeover bid, removed rubbish bags from outside the home of Roger Carr, Williams' managing director. On this occasion the investigators were spotted taking the bags in broad daylight and their vehicle registration number was reported to the police by an astute builder next door.[6]

The key question as to legality is whether or not the rubbish concerned constitutes abandoned property. In resolving this issue much will depend on satisfactory answers to the following questions:

1 Location of rubbish?
2 Type of building?
3 Who recovered the rubbish?
4 Where did the search take place?

Alternatively, one should ask whether or not there was an intention permanently to deprive the original owner of his or her rubbish.

Using these criteria, it is probably necessary to obtain a search warrant to examine rubbish stored immediately outside the rear door of a domestic residence and placed outside the back fence only on collection day. Rubbish thrown onto a communal pile behind a large multi-tenanted apartment building might not require such a warrant. It is unlikely that courts would allow 'bin searches' inside buildings even if there had been a suggestion of intent to abandon the property. The key criteria are common sense, good reconnaissance and avoiding trespass which, when combined with theft or intent to thieve, could constitute burglary.

In the USA, the recent case of The People v. Richard Whotte[7] in the Michigan Appeal Court involved rubbish searches without a warrant. It was determined that it can be legal to search rubbish and refuse its disclosure as evidence in certain circumstances. The facts of this case were that a detective was investigating a hold-up in a bar and was interviewing a possible suspect at an apartment when he noticed rubbish scattered behind the building in the garbage collection area. Among this litter he identified credit card receipts, the suspect's wedding licence, and the wallet belonging to one of the victims. All of this information was used as evidence in court and contributed to the guilty verdict. The defendant's appeal against conviction was unsuccessful.

According to Norman Butterfield, LLB: 'In this country under section 27 of the Control of Pollution Act 1974 it is an offence for anyone to sort or disturb refuse left for a local authority in a receptacle for waste provided by the local authority or at a place provided by the local authority for depositing waste.'[8] In the United Kingdom search warrants are issued only to assist in the search for specific items such as stolen property, and there is no legislation that enables a warrant to be issued to solicit information for the purposes of industrial espionage. However, it should be noted that evidence that has been illegally obtained in such a manner will not necessarily be excluded in court.

Clarification of the law occurred in a case recently reported in the *Guardian*. During the acrimonious industrial espionage war between Lord King's British Airways and Richard Branson's Virgin Atlantic, John Reilly, a private detective, was sub-contracted by an ex-SAS soldier, Stuart Francis, who was allegedly working for BA. Reilly was caught removing three black plastic bin-bags from the home of Roger Eglin, then Managing Director of the *Sunday Times*. Reilly was convicted of theft and fined £150 by Isleworth Crown Court. In the words of Judge Bernard Marder: 'An Englishman's rubbish bin is part of his castle . . . and if his black bag is violated he has the right to bring theft charges against the culprit.'[9]

The test therefore appears to be highly subjective. Thus, if an unauthorized person removed items from a waste bin, then technically this would constitute theft if the circumstances were such that the waste paper concerned was going for sale to a waste-paper collector or had been specifically left for collection by a local authority or private contractor, as in these circumstances it would not have been abandoned. Ordinarily there would be a defence against a charge of theft in that there would be a reasonable belief that the property removed under these circumstances had been abandoned by the owner, but the recent BA/Virgin case has clouded this issue somewhat. Those who engage in such activities will usually ensure that the material is returned to the area soon after the event so that they can prove that there was no 'intention to permanently deprive' the owner of his rubbish.

In conclusion, the law remains unclear and much will depend on individual circumstances. The following list of action points would no doubt be observed by anyone who chose to pursue this potentially illegal line of investigation:

1 Find out on which day and at what time the rubbish is collected to avoid wasted trips.
2 Always try to collect between 2 a.m. and 4 a.m.
3 Always 'recce' the area thoroughly – any lights on any-where, security trip-lights, dogs or cats? If you need to go onto the property, leave a bogus bag of the same type so as not to arouse suspicion.
4 Always have a reason to be there – excuses such as a sudden need for the toilet or looking for a lost item are useful, as are conducting market research, operating a mini-cab service, or simply being lost.
5 Avoid trespass wherever possible; trespass at your peril.
6 It is best to go alone, which may be easier in built-up areas. In the countryside the sound of a vehicle stopping or slowing down can easily arouse attention. Where a foray into the countryside is needed, use the following procedures:
    (a) Full reconnaissance of area
    (b) Two personnel
    (c) Assess drop-off point
    (d) Passenger leaves vehicle as car slows but does not stop
    (e) Car continues to predetermined location and waits for an agreed time. Engine is not turned off
    (f) Passenger locating rubbish moves to agreed pick-up point at predetermined time

(g) Passenger drops tell-tale object in middle of road which will be the signal to the driver to dip lights in readiness for the collection

(h) Car moves off at predetermined time with lights on full beam; lights are dipped at key point, car slows down and collects passenger and booty, and then slowly accelerates away from the location

(i) If possible, return the rubbish to the scene

AGENT RECRUITMENT

So long as we live in a world divided by profound ideological differences of outlook, there will be those on both sides who will decide at some stage in their careers to switch their allegiance

The Security Commission[10]

These words were spoken in the context of East—West tension against the background of the Cold War, but they apply equally to industrial espionage and corporate intelligence-gathering. Agents may be motivated by a variety of different means, such as sex, money, blackmail, and ideology. The latter is true even within private-sector industries where there may be environmental or pollution factors to be considered.

In his book *Traitors*, Chapman Pincher refers to MICE — Money, Ideology, Compromise and Ego — as an acronym for motivation.[11] He devotes an entire chapter to discussing the conflict of loyalty between colleagues and the industrial concern, and he stresses how loyalty can be seen as loyalty to a class, to a profession, to religion or to some sort of ideological standard, or indeed to oneself. Ideally, people likely to be influenced by such factors would be eliminated at interview stage, but circumstances change and continual monitoring is not cost-effective. Indeed, if too obvious it could become oppressive and result in an increasingly disaffected workforce and bad public relations, which could easily be exploited by the opposition.

Recruiting of agents may be effected by overt and covert methods, the exploitation of innocence and trust, or by using volunteers and professionals to carry out the work.

An overtly recruited agent will know what is at stake in terms of remuneration by cash, favours, flattery or better career prospects. Covert agents tend to act only for money or other benefits. Some might be employed as consultants to assist with a research project. Often surplus information will be requested as a 'cover' and the key information will be extracted later. Often the agent's controller will employ techniques of flattery to appeal to the agent's vanity. Classic targets of covert recruitment are management consultants and journalists, as both often have great knowledge of their areas of speciality and are often well connected. Volunteers are unusual as agents, as often their motivation will be ideological, although they are also subject to the same human weaknesses of greed and self-interest as other groups.

The exploitation of the innocent can be defined as encouraging someone to provide information without their being aware of the true situation. Typical scenarios might include meeting competitors at social events, conferences, conventions and trade shows. Targets may be staff, suppliers, clients, financial or economic journalists and professional business people.

Professional agents are trained individuals who have particular investigative or electronics skills that can be employed on an ad hoc contract basis. Among such people one will find surveillance teams, electronic counter-measure 'sweep' specialists, private detectives, and security consultants. Many of the latter are ex-special forces, Customs and Excise, intelligence services, CID or Serious Fraud Office. Included in their number one finds lawyers and accountants and people from a host of different backgrounds. Some of the larger investigative firms employ sophisticated financial detectives specializing in due-diligence enquiries, fraud investigations, corporate intelligence-gathering, kidnap and ransom negotiations, risk assessment, asset identification, and a host of other skills. Such firms can provide highly qualified and multi-lingual specialists and offer a global service.

More straightforward investigation work can be carried out by smaller firms or sole traders, and lists of such institutions and people can be found in the respective directories of the Association of British Investigators, the Institute of Professional Investigators, and the World Association of Detectives. However, it should be noted that the higher the profile of a company and the greater their portfolio of blue-chip clients, the less likely they will be to engage in 'dirty' work.

Typical targets for agents will include the following, although the list is far from exhaustive:

(a) Personnel files
(b) Board minutes
(c) Accounts records – interim reports that do not have to be filed at Companies House
(d) Memoranda
(e) Internal telephone extension directories with names
(f) Sales details
(g) New product designs
(h) Research and development
(i) Future policy proposals
(j) 'Post-it' notes – even those underneath will have the top sheet's writing impressed on them

It was Kim Philby who said that 'To betray, you must first belong'.[12] To guard against covert infiltration, it is imperative that all staff are monitored closely at all times and that thorough due-diligence enquiries are carried out to deter agent recruitment.

CHAPTER FOUR

Investigating People

Time's glory is to calm contending kings,
To unmask falsehood, and bring truth to light
William Shakespeare[1]

The investigation of an individual can take many forms and is justifiable in many ways. Employees, whether they be direct or indirect, are arguably a company's most valuable asset. They should be chosen carefully, kept happy but also monitored closely throughout their careers to ensure that there is no cause for concern, be it through negligence or misconduct. Individuals may also be of interest in the context of a potential risk assessment such as a takeover or merger and acquisition. Just how much do you know about the people? Is it enough for you to feel confident about carrying out business? Is there any point in making a bid for a company if you know that the major shareholders do not need the money, however generous your inducement might be? Any such enquiry should be complementary to corporate investigation. The normal term given to these investigations is due-diligence enquiries.

THE APPLICANT

It is always important to verify all aspects of a curriculum vitae as many applicants will 'gild the lily' to exaggerate their finer points, and some will lie blatantly or omit key aspects of their life-history. It is common to find that once a curriculum vitae has been fully checked and analysed, the applicant will look

like an overactive under-achiever. In dealing with an app
the following procedures should be followed.

(a) Ensure that the applicant completes an *application form*
on his arrival at the office and use the excuse that this is
normal procedure. In this way you can specifically design
questions that will verify his background and integrity.

(b) Ensure that the applicant does *not have a copy of his CV near
him* when completing the form and that he is supervised
during completion.

(c) The application form should detail *all addresses since school
age*, as in this way any past problems, such as bankruptcy,
county court judgements, mortgage or loan default, and
criminal antecedents, can be verified.

(d) Include a question about *directorships* and if any are listed
then check the applicant out via Companies House – did
the company fail?

(e) Ensure that *confidentiality clauses* are incorporated and that
a signed and dated declaration is made as to the truth
and honesty of all statements made on the application
form. Hesitation or a reluctance to sign may indicate
something untoward in the applicant's details.

(f) *Academic record* – ask to see the originals of all certificates
and their subject grades. In addition, contact each institution and check on grades, subjects studied, hobbies,
pursuits and general attainment. Many schools and universities or polytechnics are more than happy to give this
information over the telephone. Independent schools are
particularly keen to maintain contact with former pupils
as they are useful for future fund-raising.

(g) *Work record* – ensure that all names and addresses are
provided, as well as precise dates of employment, nature
of job description, skills and responsibilities, salary and
the reason for leaving, and corroborate these answers by
writing to the company concerned. Watch for signs of
panic or distress on the applicant's face when this kind
of detail is requested. When writing to a company, check

that it still exists at the address given via the electronic Yellow Pages or through one of the electronic data agencies such as CCN or Infolink. If you do not want the applicant to know that you are checking, then either employ a firm of investigators or consider using a dummy company or address.

(h) *Membership of trades, guilds or professional bodies* – check with the appropriate directory in your nearest reference library or call the institution up directly. They are more than happy to verify information over the telephone.

(i) *Military background* – any reference library will have copies of the *Red Book*, the Navy *Blue Book* and the *Sky Blue Book* for the Army, Navy and Royal Air Force respectively. They come in two volumes respectively, referring to existing and past members, and should be a quick reference guide as to name, rank, regiment, awards and serial number. Only in extreme security cases such as those involving the SAS, SBS or Army Intelligence in Northern Ireland will these details be excluded. It is also possible to check with the respective force's personnel records, though they will seldom give out this information without the correct Army number or the written consent of the applicant. In cases where you do not want the applicant to know that you are checking, this will be difficult. In addition, officers will often belong to one of the following clubs – the RAF Club, the Army and Navy Club, or the Cavalry and Guards Club. While these clubs will seldom, if ever, provide information to non-members, it is normally easy to access the premises with a suitable pretext or by posing as a member. Often a member's booklet will lie in the smoking-room, as well as various regimental magazines which can be a valuable source of information on various military personalities.

(j) *Criminal background.* While the Rehabilitation of Offenders Act (1974) allows certain classes of crime to lapse after set periods, some jobs will demand that full and frank disclosure be made. It is sensible to include the question 'Have you ever been convicted or sentenced for any crime in the UK or overseas? If your answer is "yes", then please provide full details of the circumstances', although any confident liar can easily write 'no' and leave matters to rest. Technically, there is nothing more one can do without possibly committing an illegal act oneself. Some individuals may choose to employ a private investigator or a security consultant to unearth the information for an agreed fee, providing them with a copy of the subject's birth certificate, his height, place of birth, father's name, and a list of recent addresses. Those who do not want to risk this line of enquiry, which could cost the investigator concerned and the perpetrator their freedom, may instead choose to scan local and national newspapers for the details of any criminal cases involving the subject. Many newspapers keep back issues, and the British Library will have copies of all local and national newspapers. Alternatively, try an electronic news database service such as Dialog or FT Profile.

(k) *Original documentation.* To reduce the risk of lies and mis-representations, insist that any applicant provides you with his birth certificate and where possible his passport and driving licence as well. Photocopies should be avoided. These documents will contain information such as names of next of kin, addresses and dates of birth. On a UK driving licence, the date of birth is found in the coded reference in the top left-hand corner of the certifi-cate.

(l) *Employer's Mutual Protection Service (EMPS).* This organiz-ation is based in the St James's area of London and, as the name suggests, offers employers a mutually beneficial service in relation to recalcitrant employees who have been dismissed for offences of dishonesty. The service operates by annual subscription and a nominal charge for each name and date of birth checked. All checks can be done on the telephone following the confirmation of a user code reference. This is a cost-effective and vitally important service for any employer.

(m) *The Office of Receiverships and Bankruptcies.* In 1991 this body relocated from London to Birmingham. The service is free and involves the completion of an application form that asks for the full name, address, date of birth and occupation of the subject. An automatic check is then carried out and any information on an existing or a discharged bankruptcy will be sent to the applicant. The service can be speeded up by using fax machines, but the normal turnaround time is three days. Unless a longer check is specifically requested, the check will normally run from 1973 to the present, and so it is always wise to check from when the subject was sixteen and thus likely to be commencing employment. Occasionally, additional information will be provided by reference to the Sir Thomas More Building of the Law Courts in London. Normally, one will need to show good reason why this information should be revealed, and the Law Courts may insist on the consent of the bankrupt person.

(n) Regarding addresses, you should consider subscribing to an *electronic database credit check service*. The four largest in the UK are CCN, Infolink, Westcott Data and Credit, and the Data and Marketing Service. This service is by subscription with a set fee charged for the number of requests made. It is useful for determining whether the subject has any county court judgements or loans listed against his name. The status of these loans or county court judgements can also be ascertained by a simple call to the help desk of the particular service chosen. For county court judgements, the additional information provided will be in the form of the name of the county court and the plaintiff's number; for loans, their status in terms of non-payment or sporadic payments. Any other information on county court judgements is obtainable only through the Register of County Court Judgements in London or at the individual county court concerned. It is unusual for the name of either party to be provided. In the USA, credit agreements are registered at state level as a Uniform Commercial Code (UCC). There are similar arrangements in many European countries. Both Infolink and CCN use the voters rolls to indicate who is living at a property, and this can be useful in identifying gay, lesbian or unmarried couples, which may be of significance in specialist areas where an employee might become the victim of blackmail.

(o) *Electronic on-line news databases*. Precise details of such databases are found in a separate chapter. Two of the more popular ones are FT Profile and Dialog. It is wise to consider a subscription service in order to run an individual's name through the system to see what is generated. Bear in mind that both positive and negative data can be of use in your intelligence-gathering.

(p) *References* should always be taken up, but consider that no applicant in his right mind would provide referees who would give him a bad or indifferent reference.

(q) *Trade or professional directories*. Check names and qualifications against entries in the directories of the institution concerned. This can be done in any good reference library or directly with the institution concerned.

(r) *Personality directories*. Typical examples of these are *Who's Who* and *The International Who's Who*, as well as the various nationally produced *Who's Who*s. A list of other useful directories can be found in Appendix 4. Once again, most good reference libraries will have these items.

(s) *Status directories*. Examples in the UK are *Debrett* and the now defunct *Burke's Peerage*. Both can be of use in checking an applicant's right or claim to a title. Luckily, in the UK the rules on primogeniture, whereby the title will only pass to the first-born son, make the job of tracing easier. In continental Europe, the lack of rules on primogeniture and the collapse of the old order through the advent of republicanism and communism have made it very difficult to confirm titles. About the only method is to consult Ruvigny's *Titled Nobility of Europe* (see Chapter 3). Be very wary of bogus counts and countesses.

(t) Check the Law Courts' *Daily Cause Lists* for the subject's name on any writs, petitions for divorce or bankruptcy and any pending cases.

(u) It is important to *corroborate any claims by the applicant to have spent time travelling around the world* or 'trekking in the Himalayas', as a four-month trip could easily be cover for time spent in prison. Ask to see the applicant's original passport, which should show all entry and exit stamps as well as visas. Do not accept visas on their own – the person concerned may have obtained the visa as a 'false flag' but may not have travelled anywhere except down to Brixton or Pentonville prisons.

At first sight these measures may seem excessive, but once the mechanics are in place the system is routine and worthwhile.

EXISTING EMPLOYEES

We have already discussed in Chapter 3 how industrial spies can be recruited. It is critical that constant reviews be made of an employee's performance, their relationships with colleagues and clients, and their overall attitudes. Be wary of resigned or distant attitudes, apathy and, in particular, excessive interest in arriving early and in working late. These are the classic times for industrial espionage, breach of confidence, or fraudulent activity.

Be wary of employees who are very close to you, such as a personal assistant to the chairman. In a recent case reported extensively in the *Sunday Times*, *The Times*, *Today*, the *Financial Times* and the *Daily Telegraph* in 1990 and 1991, a major scandal erupted over alleged industrial espionage by National Car Parks (NCP) against their rivals, Europarks. NCP had become paranoid about this new rival usurping its strong market position, which generated a turnover of £151 million and profits of

£37.5 million through control of over 650 car parks throughout the UK. In spite of this massive market lead, in 1985 NCP felt threatened when Stephen Tucker of Europarks began chasing NCP's customers in a classic and perfectly legitimate business fashion — trying to offer a better service with better terms. Europarks' success was huge, and they broke NCP's virtual monopoly at airports.

NCP's Chief Executive was Gordon Layton, who was convinced that Europarks were using underhand tactics. Layton consulted a security company called KAS, which was formed in 1986 by the founder of the Special Air Service, the late Sir David Stirling, and Ian Crooke, an ex-SAS officer. According to the *Sunday Times*, KAS produced a feasibility study suggesting various 'methods of penetration' of Europarks, including bugging and surveillance of certain key Europarks offices, and infiltration. According to the feasibility study: 'The long-term aim of this operation would be to place our operators in the Europarks hierarchy as a mole in either the London or Manchester office.' For over two years, KAS allegedly mounted a surveillance operation on Stephen Tucker and Oren Barrie, another Europarks director. KAS employed a man to get a job as a car park attendant, 'bin searches' were carried out on key people, and attempts were made to obtain Tucker's itemized mobile phone bills to find out who he was calling. There were even attempts to 'tap' telephones.

However, potentially the most serious threat came from a Europarks employee who was Stephen Tucker's personal assistant. KAS recruited a thirty-year-old former army captain called Jane Turpin for this role. Turpin allegedly provided NCP with details of how Tucker was able to undercut rivals, gave weekly briefings to NCP on Europarks' progress, stole management accounts, and also provided a wealth of information on Tucker himself. Turpin left Europarks in October 1989 without having been detected. She subsequently made an alleged confession to the *Sunday Times*. KAS went into liquidation and Stephen Tucker issued a writ against NCP claiming damages for industrial espionage, and made a formal complaint to Scotland

Yard. An out-of-court settlement followed and the civil case was dropped. However, criminal proceedings did follow and reached the Old Bailey in January 1993.[2]

(a) *Electronic monitoring*. Where your suspicions are aroused, consider employing outside security consultants to install electronic surveillance or a bug on the subject's office telephone. This is perfectly legal, and so long as it relates to his office telephone only then there will be no breach of either the Wireless Telegraphy Act (1949) or the Interception of Communications Act (1985). The details of how this can be done can be found in Chapter 9. The bug will be placed at some point on the subject's line well away from his actual telephone. This is a good method of determining whether the subject is breaching company policy or the law. The cost will be in the region of £150 to £500 per room, depending on the company or the device chosen. Non-linear devices which use radio waves tend to be more expensive and are really unnecessary as the surveillance contractor will be invited onto the premises by directors to carry out the work at a predetermined time. The monitoring of phone calls is a popular deterrent within banks' and finance houses' broking and dealing rooms where the temptations of insider dealing may never be far away.

(b) *Limit access to key areas*, such as confidential files.

(c) *Divide and rule* – only tell employees as much as they need to perform their task adequately.

(d) *Do not permit mobile computers or photocopiers* to be brought onto the premises.

(e) *Be wary* of employees working long and irregular hours.

HOW MUCH IS AN INDIVIDUAL WORTH?

The more a recession hurts, the more businesses and individuals will fail to pay their debts and litigation will follow. However, litigation is expensive and there is little point in winning an action if there are no funds left in the coffers. Such a victory will only be of the Pyrrhic variety. It is therefore becoming increasingly popular for law firms to employ private investigators or security consultants for the purposes of identifying national and international liquid and non-liquid assets – a form of preemptive strike. One of the great advantages of employing a security consultant is that the subject will normally remain unaware of what is going on and will therefore be less likely to dispose of assets. This can be useful in seeking interlocutory or Mareva injunctions and even Anton Pillar orders, which are granted by a judge to prevent the destruction of evidence.

Various newspapers know that their readers, whether motivated by envy or otherwise, like to know who is wealthy and how much they own. Thus *Forbes* magazine produces a list of the four hundred richest people in the world each October,[3] and a similar list is produced by the *Sunday Times Magazine* for the four hundred richest individuals in the United Kingdom.[4] The *Sunday Times* defines its twelve criteria for assessing wealth under the title 'The Rules of Engagement', which include the following:

1 'Wealth' refers to land, property, racehorses, art, major shareholdings in public companies, but does not include cash in the bank or small share portfolios.
2 Many landowners cannot sell their lands for legal reasons, but the values of these lands are included as the owners enjoy the benefit of them.
3 Artworks can be valued based on auction-house prices.
4 Family-held trusts and equity portfolios are very hard to research for value.

5 Many company directors with large equity holdings in their own companies would be unlikely to be able to sell them at their market price and in some cases where they are very substantial, perhaps not at all. In addition, share prices can fluctuate wildly even in a single day of trading.
6 Land can be valued using information from estate agents and occasional regional surveys in newspapers.
7 Shares in publicly quoted companies can be valued at the 'stock exchange' price but those of private companies cannot. How can shares in private companies be valued? As a rule of thumb you should either compare the private company with a comparably sized publicly quoted company (PLC) or, alternatively, estimate the total shares in issue as being worth 12.5 times the most recent post-tax figure. However, this multiplication will only apply to larger companies.

The *Sunday Times* was primarily interested in typical aristocratic sources of wealth, such as rural land and sporting rights, as their targets were UK-based wealthy people.

It is also useful to check national and local newspapers for references to the assets of individuals as, while not always referring to actual aggregate cash-worth figures, articles may mention yachts, houses in London and the country, and also properties overseas. Enquiries can be made manually or on-line with an electronic news database.

CREDIT DATABASE SOURCES

Prominent UK examples are Infolink, CCN, Westcott Data and Credit, and the Data Marketing Service. CCN holds thirty million items of financial information and 2.5 million 'personal profiles'. These systems will provide the enquirer with details of loans, their size, regularity of payment and their status. If a subject is massively in debt, then there is little point in seizing non-existent liquid assets.

ACCOUNTS AND FINANCIAL DATA ANALYSIS

Details of shareholdings, dividend payments and annual directors' remuneration, which will include base salary plus benefits such as a car, private health and gymnasium and pension schemes, can be found by analysing the company's annual returns. In addition, details of other company directorships must be provided according to statute, and this can lead to further information regarding annual salary.

LAND REGISTRY/ESTATE AGENTS

Once an address has been determined, check to see who owns the property, whether the property is subject to any charges or encumbrances, and establish the value by enquiring about comparable properties with estate agents. If the property is mortgaged, it is likely that the mortgage will be for at least £30,000 to take advantage of mortgage interest relief at source (Miras). The Land Registry documents will not provide details of the outstanding mortgage. To obtain this information you must employ underhand methods such as inventing a pretext – often people will indicate the bands into which their mortgage falls, though seldom the precise figure.

RUBBISH COLLECTION AND COLLATION

Chapter 3 covers this topic in detail. It can be very useful where abandoned property includes bank account details, statements, credit card slips and other financial paraphernalia such as pay slips and pension fund information.

PHYSICAL INSPECTIONS/
SURVEILLANCE

This can be useful to assess spending habits, indications of gambling, the subject's dress, vehicle types and index numbers, evidence of boats, the condition of the house, estimated cost of upkeep, schools, numbers of children, domestic staff, existence of a conservatory or swimming-pool, and the condition of the garden or outbuildings. The law of trespass in the UK is confined to the civil courts unless it is linked to theft or an intent to steal, in which case it becomes burglary. Thus, looking through windows to identify furnishings and the number of rooms will not cause a problem. In addition, there is no law against using pretexts to gain entry to premises; among the more popular are posing as a market researcher, charity worker, or antique dealer.

BANK AND CREDIT CARD DETAILS

If rubbish expeditions do not succeed in revealing bank balances or details of account numbers, it is worth considering using a security consultant who may have access to gas, water and electricity companies and the local authority with respect to the community charge, and will be able to establish whether payment has been made by standing order or by direct debit. If so, this will reveal the bank account number and the name and address of the bank. Where this is not possible the more expert private investigation firms will often be able to get bank and credit card details by using 'false flag' phone calls. Many of these organizations will also know the codes banks use unofficially to authenticate telephone enquiries from other branches.[5]

If you know the credit card number and have additional information on the subject such as full name, date of birth, address and telephone numbers of home and work, and, in the case of a joint credit card, the name of the spouse, this will normally be enough to convince the credit card company that you are the legitimate user. An alternative method is to pretend that you are a retail outfit using the particular card in question, and by calling a special telephone number (which you can normally pick up by listening to a transaction involving your own card) you will be told whether the credit card company is prepared to authorize a transaction of that particular size. The company will then issue an authorization number.

INLAND REVENUE/DEPARTMENT OF SOCIAL SECURITY RECORDS

These records can be critical in asset identification, but the information is confidential and so it is best, if considering this option, to employ a sub-contractor in such a way that you can disclaim responsibility if things go wrong. Typical information provided would be:

(a) Gross salary less tax = net salary
(b) National insurance number
(c) Type of income tax – Schedule DI, DII, DIII or Schedule E.
(d) Details of capital gains and any tax thereon
(e) Whether the subject is under investigation by the Inland Revenue
(f) Whether the subject is receiving unemployment benefit or income support
(g) Details of the subject's accountants or tax consultants including their address which could lead to more information by means of a rubbish expedition

MISCELLANEOUS

Examples would include wife's income or family wealth or a recent windfall from an inheritance. Checks on the latter can be made with the Wills and Probate Office at Somerset House in the Strand. It is also wise to check Lloyd's Register or *Debrett's Register of Yachts* for details of yachts in the name of the subject. However, both of these registers are limited as both rely on voluntary entries, and the latter ceased publication in 1985.

ESTABLISHING NET WORTH

According to C. Griffiths in *International Criminal Police Review*, fraud investigators use a four-stage formula for establishing the net worth of an individual, namely:

(a) Assets – liabilities = net worth
(b) Net worth – previous year's net worth = annual net worth growth
(c) Annual net worth growth living expenses = income
(d) Income – legal or known sources = illegal or unknown sources[6]

Once the formula has been applied the investigator will seek to uncover assets from these unknown or illegal sources.

PUTTING FLESH ON A SKELETON

No man is truly invisible. Everyone has an identity and sometimes the new identity is drastically different from the former. How does one go about creating people from just a name? The sheer geographic mobility and internationalization of the modern world have made this job harder, but by no means impossible. The key is common sense and logical deduction. For example:

FACT	QUESTION	SOLUTION	RESULTS
All humans are born.	Estimate age of subject via visual id, job status, circle of friends, hobbies, military rank, etc.	Check the Gen. Register of births & deaths.	Father's name. Mother's names, including maiden name. Full name of subject. Precise date of birth. Father's occupation and address of family.
In the UK all children attend school from 5–16. Unless private, the schools are local to the family residence.	Where was address at time of birth? Where is address now?	Check all local schools for the name of the subject. Try local authority records.	Details on subject such as brothers and sisters and qualifications. Where did they go after school — university, the military or polytechnic?
Most fathers likely to work.	Did he belong to a profession?	Check all appropriate directories historically.	Further biographical details on the family.
Most people have a phone.	Check phone books for addresses.	Use CCN or Infolink methods which rely on the Voters Roll.	Names of all voters, details of unpaid county court judgements and loans.
Many people in the UK are baptized as Christians. Many marry in churches.	If the subject is or was a member of the Church of England, can you access the records?	Try the Mormon church's records in South Kensington, London or the church local to the place of birth.	Details of baptisms, confirmations, marriages and deaths.

CHAPTER FIVE

Investigating Companies

They lard their lean books with the fat of others'
work

Democritus[1]

The investigation of companies is the classic aim of industrial
espionage or 'competitor analysis'. In the United Kingdom a
company is normally a public limited company, a limited company, or a company limited by guarantee. The latter is generally an anachronism, and for the purposes of this study only
the former two types will be discussed. One of the great disad-
vantages of being limited, and thus having limited liability if
business matters go wrong, is the necessity to sacrifice information to the public domain. However, this can be done in
such a way as to minimize publicity.

It is common for companies to keep intelligence files on
business opponents. They will do this by accessing and evaluating publicly available data from Companies House, using press
reports, and building up profiles based on history, rumour,
conjecture, logical deduction, supposition and fact. But it is
not just rival companies or hostile governments who wish to
glean this information. Lawyers, accountants, management
consultants, head-hunters, market analysts and risk arbitra-
geurs all play their part in corporate intelligence-gathering.
The increased incidence of mergers and acquisitions in the
1980s caused a massive growth in this area.

Financial discipline is vital, and includes not only key
accounting ratios and the mastery of company methodology
but also a capacity for lateral thought processes and preemptive

speculation. There are myriad reasons why people enter business and profit maximization is but one of them. The following formula must always be borne in mind:

```
COLLECT → SORT → ANALYSE → DEDUCE
```

To find out whether a company is registered, you should consider the following methods:

1 Yellow Pages (manual and electronic). In the UK the Electronic Yellow Pages cover 1.8 million businesses in sixty-six regional editions.
2 Electronic databases such as CCN and Infolink.
3 Enquiry agents such as Jordan's or Dun and Bradstreet. The latter covers 1.5 million businesses in twenty-nine different countries. In the USA, Dun and Bradstreet have a business directory that covers 8.4 million businesses and a market identifiers service with extra information on 2.4 million of these same companies.
4 Manual enquiry via Companies House and the microfiche system.
5 Extel, which uses annual reports, six-monthly statements and any company announcements of a 'price sensitive nature', although it only covers quoted companies (PLCs).
6 Kompass, which is a three-volume, annually produced book that provides more detailed basic information on companies.

A company which is registered in a particular area of the world will have to comply with that country's or region's duties of disclosure as regards their published accounts. These can vary wildly. Chapter 7 deals with the merits of offshore company registration. In the UK, if the company concerned is a Public Limited Liability Company (PLC) then it needs to attract financial support from the general public by styling itself as attractive to potential investors and existing equity holders. In addition, PLCs must comply specifically with the listing regulations of the Stock Exchange which require a high level of disclosure and also seek to avoid insider dealing through the use of price-sensitive information.

In the UK, the annual returns of a limited liability company will reveal the following:

(a) Balance sheet
(b) Profit and loss account
(c) Statement of the source and application of funds
(d) Managing director's report
(e) The registered office of the company
(f) The register of members' location
(g) The company directors and secretary
(h) Share interests of directors and secretary as well as other shareholdings
(i) Mortgages and charges relating to the company
(j) The company's register of debentures
(k) The company's bankers (in a private limited company these are invariably the same as those of the key director)

Additional information will include the company's constitution in the form of the Memorandum and the Articles of Association which are generally a standard boiler-plate but can be individualized according to taste.

THE FORENSIC ACCOUNTANT

Accountancy is a discipline that collects all of the available data on a company or an industry and presents the information in financial terms to managers and politicians. The skill in evaluating these figures comes from financial analysis, but such skill is not confined to the accountant. Fluency in the interpretation of accounts or financial analysis does not require a professional qualification in accountancy, as you simply need to understand the nature and context of various accounting statements and their interrelationship with one another.

Dates are important in terms of looking at the chronology of a company's affairs, but it should be remembered that accounts are generally time-specific while businesses are dynamic and situations can change very quickly. Thus, if a debtor pays off his debt, a view of the accounts on the next day will show an automatic change in the picture of the firm's possessions. Cash will have increased and the previous day's balance sheet will not accurately reflect the firm's current possessions.

A crucial distinction to understand in basic financial analysis is that between capital expenditure and revenue expenditure. Capital expenditure will appear in the balance sheet as fixed assets and may be defined as the expenditure incurred on the acquisition of 'permanent' assets. Examples would include industrial buildings, plant and machinery, vehicles, some loose tools, and modifications of existing assets. The intent of the spender is for the asset to survive longer than a single accounting period. On the other hand, revenue expenditure represents a short-term commitment with no permanence, such as rent, the recently introduced uniform business rate, insurance, salaries, repair work, maintenance costs, licences, oil and gasoline. Thus it represents the costs of goods and services that are entirely consumed in the production processes of the current accounting period. As such this expenditure will always appear in the profit and loss account.

Another fundamental factor to understand is the distinction between income and expenditure. Income means the value of sales achieved by the business during the appropriate accounting period. The sum total of sales achieved should tally with the total value of the goods despatched to customers from the factory or shop during the same accounting period. Expenditure refers to the total cost of the resources used up during the accounting period.

The figures found within a set of financial statements will provide sufficient information for interested parties, using accounting ratios, to gain a greater insight into the affairs of an organization. The more markets compete, the more analysts and investigators will find it desirable to compare one company's performance with another's, especially with companies operating in the same areas. To ensure accuracy and objectivity, various accounting ratios are used.

Accounting ratios

1 Return on capital employed

This represents pre-tax profit and is used to evaluate investment in any venture. It is an overall average measure of a company's efficiency in utilizing its assets and is expressed as a percentage. An analogy can be drawn with a decision as to whether to put money into a building society or National Savings Bonds, as here the rate of return is the interest generated by the capital investment. Return on capital employed (ROCE) is also known as the primary ratio or the return on investment (ROI).

2 Mark-up/return on sales

This is a term that expresses net profit as a percentage of the value of sales achieved during the accounting period. The mark-up on an individual sale refers to the anticipated level of gross profit. The net profit shown in the profit and loss account represents the figure for total net mark-up. Finally, the return on sales minus the net profit mark-up represents a measure of the cost efficiency of the company throughout its entire manufacturing and distribution process. The ratio is often known as the return on sales ratio (ROSR).

3 Turnover on capital employed

A measure of the efficiency of the available assets used to produce output, this ratio demonstrates the extent to which a company's physical assets can be used to produce goods for sale. Thus, a firm with an efficient production flow on the shop floor will have a greater output than an inefficient work area. The ratio is often known as the asset utilization ratio (AUR).

These first three accounting ratios correlate to represent the preliminary analysis of a company's activities as follows:

$$\text{Return on capital employed} = \text{net profit on sales} \times \text{Turnover of capital employed.}$$

which can be fully expressed by the equation:

$$\frac{\text{Profit} \times 100}{\text{Capital employed}} = \frac{\text{Profit} \times 100}{\text{Sales}} \times \frac{\text{Sales}}{\text{Capital employed}}$$

The ROCE formula is a very popular financial analysis indicator and is used widely in comparisons of the various profits of different firms and industries. Therefore the figures for the accounting profit and the capital employed sums can be drastically altered by alternative methods of valuing assets, such as profit after tax, pre-tax profit, profit after tax and interest, and pre-tax profit and depreciation.

In seeking to avoid insularity and the risks of managers budgeting and working towards conflicting objectives, many firms now adopt integrated schemes of ratios which are known as pyramid ratios. The equation above is but one example of a pyramid – ROCE above and supported by ROSR and AUR underneath.

4 Solvency

These formulae are used to enable a company to indicate its ability to meet the demands of its creditors:

$$\text{Working capital} = \text{Current assets} - \text{current liabilities}$$

$$\text{Working capital ratio} = \frac{\text{Current assets}}{\text{Current liabilities}}$$

If you are interested only in the solvency of liquid assets, then you should use the *liquidity ratio*:

$$\frac{\text{Current assets} - \text{Stocks}}{\text{Current liabilities}}$$

5 Stock turnover ratios

These ratios are used to analyse inventory movement and to determine how long an average stock item has remained with the firm. The following maxim should be used: a larger rate of turnover means a smaller risk of lost value while goods remain under the manufacturer's control.

$$\frac{\text{Cost of materials used}}{\text{Average stock of raw materials}} = \frac{X}{Y} = Z \text{ times in period}$$

$$\frac{\text{Period of account}}{Z} = Za \text{ days}$$

Is the time-scale reasonable? This is a highly subjective test and in determining the answer you should consider how long it takes to obtain new stocks and the size of your order.

The *rate for work in progress* is calculated using the following ratio:

$$\frac{\text{Cost of goods manufactured}}{\text{Average stock of work in progress}} = \frac{X}{Y} = Z \text{ period}$$

$$\frac{\text{Period of account}}{Z} = Za \text{ days}$$

To ensure that this ratio is maintained at acceptably low levels, the target firm should have an efficient production control system and a good shop-floor layout. The investigator might consider using surveillance to assess this situation.

The turnover rate of finished goods is represented by the following ratio:

$$\frac{\text{Cost of sales}}{\text{Average cost of finished goods}} = \frac{X}{Y} = Z \text{ times in the account period}$$

$$\frac{\text{Period of account}}{Z} = Za \text{ days}$$

This ratio indicates demand for the goods and the efficiency of the methods of inspection, packaging and distribution.

6 The evaluation of a business

A firm or industry's earning power and dividend can be expressed in yield percentages which are often used by analysts to assess the worth of the business. Many of the ratios discussed earlier in this chapter will be used by analysts for this purpose.

The financial analyst will not necessarily always adopt the same approach in his analysis and what is stressed and the conclusions reached will depend on the motivation of the investigation. The newspapers constantly refer to the views of analysts, and barely a day passes without one or more being interviewed on television. Thus a firm or an entire industry will often be analysed for potential takeovers or mergers and acquisitions. Typical questions asked by analysts will include how much capitalization a company has, tax considerations, any likely problems with anti-trust regulations, the best form of financing to consummate the deal (bonds, new stock offer, stock swap, straight cash or a combination), and what is the proper price to offer for the target stock, the price that will persuade shareholders to sell and will still make the deal profitable for the acquirer.

A classic example of evaluating business worth is when a bank responds to a request for an overdraft or a loan. In such a case the following information from the publicly available accounts will influence the decision of the lender:

1 Any security in the form of permanent or fixed assets for the loan's liquidation
2 Any income security to meet loan charges
3 A guaranteed management succession to give the security of implementation
4 The growth, development and continuance of the company over the next decade

Furthermore, an examination of a firm by a potential creditor for a future supply of goods would focus on the liquidity state of that firm – can the firm pay its short-term debts over the forthcoming year? Potential shareholders will also be interested in the company as they hope for dividends on a regular and increasing basis. The criterion used by the shareholder is expressed in terms of income received or the corporate net earning power of the company to himself after tax.

7 Dividend value

To show the actual gross (pre-corporation tax) return on the share's purchase price one uses the following ratio:

$$\frac{\text{Dividend per share} \times 100}{\text{Market price per share}} = \text{Gross yield per cent}$$

As the market price of a share not infrequently differs from its nominal value, any dividend paid on a share must be related to the purchase price of that share. Thus, the value of the dividend is compared with the price of the share on the Stock Exchange List on a set day.

While useful in analysis, dividends represent only part of the return to the successful investor. The value of the total profits after tax provides a far more valuable indication of worth, as it reveals the total sum of profits actually available to the business. To generate a return on an investment, the prospective investor must look at the post-corporation tax earnings. This will be the value bought when purchasing a share and is represented by the formula:

$$\frac{\text{Earnings per share} \times 100}{\text{Market price per share}}$$

These indices of investment worth refer primarily to ordinary shares which bear most of the risk in a firm's capital. Thus, once post-corporation tax earnings have been assessed, any sums that are due for preference shareholders' dividends will be deducted. The remaining figure will be divided by the number of ordinary shares in issue to determine the available earnings per ordinary share.

8 The price/earnings ratio

This is popular with property valuers who apply a method of valuation that is contingent upon the earnings which the property in question can obtain. The ratio is found when the Stock Exchange price is divided by the earnings per share:

$$\frac{\text{Market price/share}}{\text{Earnings per share}} = \frac{X}{Y} = Z$$

The rationale of the price/earnings ratio is that it provides the precise number of years over which a company's earnings per share will repay the present market price of buying that share. As a result, an analogy can be made with the straight-line method of depreciation. This is known as time capitalization. Although related to the gross earnings index, the price/earnings ratio gives a monetary value and time-scale to the relationship between earnings and share price.

9 Dividend yield

This is expressed by the formula:

$$\frac{\text{Dividend per share} \times 100}{\text{Market price per share}}$$

Popular with market analysts and corporate raiders, this information is found each day in the *Financial Times* and *Wall Street Journal*. Another useful piece of information is dividend cover, which provides an indication of the company's present capacity to repeat the most recent dividends. Dividend cover is a very useful index as it provides the investor with details of the extent to which retained earnings have exceeded the dividend allocation. In addition, it can show if the company's directors have had any problems in declaring a dividend from earnings.

PRESS COMMENT

Virtually every trade, profession or industry has its own specialist press, and many of the more respectable newspapers pass comment at some time on prominent individuals, companies or industries, as well as providing details of recruitment advertisements and new-product advertisements. While it is possible to scavenge in local and national press libraries, this is often time-consuming. Far better is to join an electronic on-line news database service such as FT Profile, Dialog or Nexis. This is discussed more fully in Chapter 2.

CREDIT CHECKS

Examples of credit checks have already been discussed in Chapter 4. Organizations offering this service include Jordan's, Dun and Bradstreet, Standard and Poor Corporation, Moody's, and Infolink. Banks tend to subscribe to their own specialist credit agencies such as Thomson Bankwatch and IBCA Banking Analysis.

TRADE DIRECTORY ENTRIES

Trade directory entries are useful information sources. Companies are often more than willing to subscribe to these publications as it helps them to market their products. The advantages for the investigator are that they are often inexpensive and readily available in reference libraries. Unfortunately, the information is often brief, out of date, and selective in that the company concerned discloses only what it wants you to see as part of their marketing strategy.

PRODUCT INFORMATION

Product information as a source is invariably subjective and an element of 'journalistic licence' will normally be employed by the firm as part of its sales policy. However, sales literature, advertisements, brochures, and price lists are invariably readily available with only a simple pretext necessary to gain information. Occasionally the brochures will give away the names of satisfied customers, which may help to indicate how and where the firm is pitching for its business.

THE MARKET ANALYST

The marriage of the stockbroker and the stockjobber in the mid-1980s produced the market analyst, who will often specialize in a particular type of company or industry. They look at fundamentals such as recent stock price ranges, dividends, performance ratios, and, in terms of analysing a potential merger, they will study all the recent acquisitions within the given industry, note all the premiums that were paid above market, and check all the multiples of book value and earnings to identify specific elements, such as the types of compensation, that were critical to those past transactions. Analysts are often bound by strict confidentiality clauses and their services are not cheap. It is a good idea to befriend one or more of them and exchange information on a tit-for-tat basis. This is popular among investigative journalists.

LAND

Statutory records will supply the company's addresses, which may include its registered office, the private addresses of various directors and the company secretary, the identity of shareholders, and also a register dealing with any mortgages or charges on land or property. The latter can be significant, as such charges may suggest urgent refinancing. Any address can then be investigated further through enquiries at the Land Registry and valuations made with local estate agents. A physical inspection of the office may be useful to establish furnishings, state of premises, size of car park, types of company cars, the existence of ventilation ducts and false walls (important in any future electronic surveillance), the number of telephone lines being used by the firm, the type of neighbourhood, as well as the way in which rubbish is collected. Plans may be drawn up quite legally and discreetly using a covert camera bag for close-up internal photographs and wide-angle, zoom and telephoto photography for other evidence.

BIOGRAPHICAL CLUES

Biographical clues can be a useful source of information. Chapter 4 deals with this subject more fully, but briefly statutory records will reveal the full names, addresses, dates of birth, signatures, other company directorships, titles, maiden names and any professional qualifications of key personnel. In addition, it is often possible to ascertain directors' remuneration from the notes in the annual accounts, as well as the value of shares in relation to any annual dividend payments.

ANNUAL ACCOUNTS

A company's annual accounts can also be useful for finding random clues which may include details of the company's accountants, its registered office, subsidiaries, and occasionally details of its PR firm or advertising agency and its lawyers. The Chairman's statement can be a revealing source of information.

CHAPTER SIX

Investigating Products

... they come not single spies but in battalions
William Shakespeare[1]

The media are full of stories of thefts from factories, ware-houses and showrooms. The more popular targets among com-panies are computer hardware and software manufacturers, the audio and pharmaceutical industries, but they also extend to the haute couture industry – in 1992, Zandra Rhodes, the famous dress designer, had her London showrooms raided. The theft of high-technology products and their illegal copying is popular throughout the world, but especially in Far Eastern territories such as Hong Kong, Taiwan, South Korea and Singa-pore. Indeed, there is a well-known story about the innovative Tissot 'Rockwatch' in the 1980s which some sources claim was copied in Hong Kong even before the original was produced. While this is a popular story, the author has found no evidence that it is true. The copying of products and the legal conse-quences are covered by intellectual property law, which embraces the breach of trademarks, copyright and patents through the Trademarks Act (1937) and the Design, Copyright and Patents Act (1988) and various international codes and regulations to which the UK is a signatory. In addition, the UK common-law remedies of breach of confidence and the tort of passing off provide non-statutory remedies. Yet this presupposes that the products and research and development have been stolen or obtained in the first place. A great deal of information can be gleaned by overt but discreet methods of corporate intelligence-gathering.

PATENTS

When any new process, product or system is developed, it is wise to register the development with the UK Patents Office as, if the product or process is accepted, this will provide statutory 'protection' against contravention by way of deterrence and damages. Under UK patent legislation, a patent will last for up to twenty years provided that all the fees are paid within the correct time-scales. An invention must be new, involve an inventive step, be capable of industrial application and not be 'excluded' on the basis that it is simply a mathematical method, a scientific discovery, a design, or an aesthetic creation.

The inventor seeking the patent will initially file his application with the Patent Office, including a full description of the invention. This description should be couched in terms enabling it to be understood by someone wishing to use the patent. The date of filing is the date used to assess the product's 'newness', and the claim is put through an initial check by a patent officer to confirm that the invention is genuinely new. If so, it is then published as a valid claim and is now available for public inspection. The examiner will subject the claim to a full investigation to ensure that it satisfies the criteria of the 1988 Act and, if so, the grant of patent will follow. Strict time limits apply to the granting of patents. There is an overall time limit of four and a half years from filing for the patent application to satisfy all the statutory requirements.

A patent is open to public inspection as part of its 'trial run period' and even when it has been accepted. You can inspect the Patent Office register yourself, or arrange for the Patent Office search and advisory service to do it for you. In addition, there are numerous patent-related electronic on-line databases available. Details can be obtained from a reference library or from the UK Patent Office. This should be the first stage in overt corporate intelligence-gathering. Indeed, the Patent Office itself invites consultation by announcing in one of its publications: 'Patents are . . . an ideal vehicle for monitoring the activities of a competitor.'

DOCUMENTARY ANALYSIS – PAPER AND ELECTRONIC

As a rule of thumb, the more scientific or technologically oriented the subject, the greater the chance of the information required being contained on an electronic on-line database. Appendix 3 details some of the various types of on-line database systems and their specialities. In using these on-line systems, the cost factor is as important as knowledge of which system suits you best and proficiency in accessing the information. Many companies also produce literature on their products and certain journals specialize in discussing new products.

TRADE SHOWS

These are perfect arenas for gleaning information on product ranges and variety. Indeed, Colonel General Mikhailov, Head of the Soviet GRU, said recently: 'The GRU is interested in all new developments in the West . . . although the old methods of stealing are never used now. Nowadays our lives are so full of information . . . we take magazines, we send people openly to exhibitions, conferences and air shows.'[2]

Every major industrialized centre will host such trade exhibitions throughout the year, and they are normally international in scope. A prime example in 1992 was the Expo Exhibition in Seville. Such shows are full of marketing and sales people who are more than happy to thrust product details, specifications and price lists into your hands, and will normally provide you with additional in-depth information by means of a 'sales introduction'. An introduction to their mailing list will normally mean that the enquirer will have a continuous up-date of information on existing and new products as soon as they leave the printing press. Any aspiring industrial spy should seek to bypass the front men and women on the sales stalls and establish contact with the experts at the back. To do this one should know enough about the industry to impress the front line and thus gain access to the rear echelon.

SURVEILLANCE

By close analysis of a working area, its geography, architecture and design, rubbish distribution methods, and communications lines, it is possible to build up an intelligent picture of what is being produced and in what quantities and of what quality. The advantages of rubbish collection have already been discussed in an earlier chapter. Often suppliers' names or brand names will appear on containers, which can assist in establishing sources and likely products. In addition, scientific analysis of pollutants and fuels can greatly assist in corporate intelligence-gathering, and the various environmental groups often experiment on deposits they collect from allegedly heavy-pollutant industries. In his book *Competitor Intelligence*, Leonard M. Fuld, who runs a competitor intelligence agency called Information Data Search Inc. in Cambridge, Massachusetts, provides a complete checklist for plant and site inspection.[3]

Aerial surveillance is of particular use when a new factory plant is under construction. An example of this occurred in 1968 when a construction crew who were building a new methanol plant for Du Pont in Beaumont, Texas noticed a plane flying above them. It transpired that the plane had been hired by competitors to penetrate the still-incomplete roof of the plant and thereby reveal details of a new industrial system being developed. The photographers argued that they were flying in public airspace and so anything they saw was in the public domain.[4]

Under English law there is no civil remedy to prevent unauthorized photography per se. In Baron Bernstein of Leigh v. Seaviews and General Ltd (1977), the defendant had taken aerial photographs of the plaintiff's property. It was determined that no trespass had been committed as the plaintiff did not own the airspace over his land. Presumably the result would have been different had the defendant conducted persistent low-level flights over the plaintiff's land, as this may have constituted a nuisance.

The impotence of the English legal system regarding the law of privacy was further evidenced in the case of Kaye v. Robinson (1990), where the TV star Gordon Kaye had to call on security guards to remove two over-zealous journalists from his private hospital room.

LOGICAL DEDUCTION – COMPLETING THE EQUATION

This book began with the short mathematical example of 2 + 2 = ? The answer was 'it depends', and reasons were given as to why the answer had to be inconclusive. Finding what something depends on is a key element in intelligence-gathering and involves anticipating an event. Hugo Cornwall[5] refers to two types of forecasting – anticipatory, which starts from the present and extrapolates to the future, and normative, which will identify a desired objective and then work retrospectively to see what is needed to achieve it.

An example of educated guesswork based on logical deduction occurred when aerial photography of Soviet ships bound for Cuba during the Cuban Missile Crisis indicated to CIA officials that numerous crates held on the decks of the ships contained aircraft and missile components. The CIA termed this practice 'crateology'.

BENCH-MARKING

More commonly known in some countries as reverse engineering, bench-marking can be defined as identifying the crucial ideas behind a product but utilizing them to develop something novel, distinctive and cost-effective. During the late 1970s, the Japanese giant Canon introduced a photocopier that was cheaper than Xerox's comparable machine. This had appalling consequences for Xerox, who saw their market share in photo-copiers shrink from forty-nine per cent to twenty-two per cent in just a few years. Xerox decided to 'bench-mark' Canon's machine and by so doing managed to arrest the slide in their market share. Bench-marking has now entered the service arena and affects sales, billing, marketing and engineering. In the words of Xerox CEO David T. Kearns: 'Bench-marking provides insights into new ways of doing business and challenges business's usual methods.'[6] Reverse engineering has also helped Ford develop the highly successful Taurus and Sable motor vehicles in the United States.

The system differs from counterfeiting or the copying of a product and passing it off as genuine in that reverse engineering strives to economize on development costs and is quite legal, although often the demarcation lines between classic counterfeiting and reverse engineering become blurred. These practices were often used by the countries of the old Warsaw Pact.

CHAPTER SEVEN

Hide and Seek – The Use of Offshore Havens

> . . . secrecy is as essential to intelligence as vestments to a Mass, or darkness to a spiritualist seance, and must be maintained, quite irrespective of whether or not it serves any purpose
>
> Malcolm Muggeridge[1]

An increasingly popular method of conducting international business is through the vehicle of an offshore entity such as a company, bank, trust fund or insurance company. A wide variety of countries and principalities in the world offer this service, which can bring with it the four great advantages of political stability, tax avoidance, asset protection, and varying degrees of discretion depending on local rules. An offshore company can range from an international trading company to a company specializing in the administration of offshore funds for firms dealing with investments and property.

Within the classified pages of the sensible daily and Sunday newspapers one can find various companies offering different divisions for different types of offshore entity. Thus, there will normally be a corporate services division which will provide the registered office, registered agents, directors and company secretary as required, and all compliance work relating to annual returns and tax filing. There will normally be both an accountancy services division and a commercial services division which will operate bank accounts, arrange for the printing of invoices and stationery, the notarizing of documents, and transfer pricing. In addition, there will be a trust division which will operate both corporate and individual trusts as trustees on the instructions of the settlor of the trust and administer the trust instrument for the benefit of the beneficiaries.

OFFSHORE TRUSTS

The main advantages of an offshore trust fund are confidentiality, tax avoidance, the protection of assets from creditors, hostile spouses and bad publicity, and the elimination of commercial risks such as expropriation or devaluation.

The key to offshore trusts in the context of this book is confidentiality, and if the settlor prefers anonymity, the trust can be signed and executed under seal by the trustees alone. An added advantage of an offshore trust fund is that there is often no requirement for trustees to file trust accounts with the local tax authority.

While there are four types of trust – express, implied, resulting and discretionary – it is the latter which is the most popular. Discretionary trusts are also known as asset protection trusts for this very reason. Such trusts provide excellent vehicles for wealthy individuals, expatriates and international business people to 'hide' their assets from the Inland Revenue, the press and their creditors.

OFFSHORE BANKING

A concomitant of offshore companies and trust funds are offshore banks which carry out banking and financial activities in an environment that is essentially free of fiscal and exchange controls and oppressive bank regulations. An example of the profusion of offshore banks is evidenced by the current existence of over 560 banks in Georgetown, the capital of the Cayman Islands – a capital that is only the size of a small English market town.

Offshore banks are often formed as a subsidiary of a domestic or an international bank for the following reasons:

(a) To supplement offshore trusts and companies.
(b) Tax avoidance.
(c) Secrecy.
(d) They accept deposits from anyone. The geography of the Caribbean is particularly useful in this respect as the region is close to Central and South American countries, rich in their 'narco-dollars', and also to the United States, the bulwark of the mighty dollar.
(e) Avoiding debt-equity ratios and lending restrictions in the heavily regulated areas of the banking world.
(f) To handle banking transactions such as international syndicated loans which rely on different banks in various parts of the world.
(g) To handle external borrowing.
(h) To consolidate inter-group finance.
(i) Discounting or factoring of inter-group loans.
(j) Leasing of equipment through an offshore-based finance company to fund group asset acquisitions.
(k) To avoid exchange controls through speed, freedom and flexibility.
(l) Savings in tax can mean better interest rates.
(m) Having a currency management centre brings flexible and tax-efficient methods of controlling Forex (foreign exchange) exposure for a corporate group.
(n) Anonymity.
(o) Minimal reporting requirements.
(p) Political and economic stability.
(q) Good communications.
(r) Proximity to business expertise.
(s) No unions.

It is imperative that the management and control of the overseas bank are not exercised within the domestic jurisdiction of any part of the corporate group to avoid the risks of tax and banking regulations. Management and control must be carried out offshore and can be in-house or delegated to specialized locals. Offshore banking activities are similar to those of any other type of banking organization, but they specialize in inter-group lending, foreign currency management, lease finance, factoring and secrecy. Numbered accounts are available and, of course, absolute discretion is guaranteed. Overseas banks are useful as they often know considerably more about business than would the average institution or individual by virtue of their experience of the risk analysis of loan portfolios. In some cases the bank will actually be linked to its client companies. Therefore they represent excellent targets for enquiries, with or without secrecy laws.

CAPTIVE INSURANCE COMPANIES

Another popular entity is the captive insurance company, which can be defined as a subsidiary of another company that is wholly owned by a non-insurance company and which conducts business exclusively to underwrite the insurable risks of its parent or its associated companies. Captive insurance companies represent self-insurance, or the concept of insuring risks by internal methods rather than in the market-place.

This form of self-insurance is undertaken by appropriating funds from a company's annual net profits to create provisions against losses that are not covered by commercial insurance underwriters.

Captive insurance cover is funded from within the group itself. As a result, structural and taxation problems must be considered. While insurance premiums are tax-deductible irrespective of the type of business of the recipient, self-insurance that is created by means of internally funded reserve provisions will seldom produce tax deductions until losses are shown. Thus, by using a captive insurance company, one can crystallize self-insurance into a distinctive corporate entity. Captive insurance schemes come in four varieties — pure captive, reciprocal captive, mutual captive, and pure captive and reinsurer. Professional advice should be sought before setting up such a scheme.

The reasons why captive insurance companies are sought are myriad, but the more popular advantages are as follows:

1 Insurance cost savings.
2 Flexibility – many insurance policies have to be standardized, but a captive can be designed for you.
3 'Overkill' in other policies – a corporate group may discover that with the expansion of its operations, a proportionately larger number of individual risks are being insured unnecessarily.
4 Using reinsurance in conjunction with a captive insurance company can aid the cash flow of the corporate group. Furthermore, the captive can assist the group's cash flow by deciding when annual premiums should be paid by group members.
5 Tax savings.
6 Funds are amassed under the control of the corporate group.
7 It can be easier to sort out insurance claims.
8 'Keeping it in the family' – avoiding leaving 'footprints' for an aspiring investigator which can happen when there is an extended line and too many people are involved. By utilizing captive insurance companies and limiting reinsurance, one can minimize market knowledge and media interest. The downside is that whoever owns the captive will bear all the risks.

Other reasons for choosing offshore havens in which to base companies or interests are to utilize 'confirming houses', whereby import/export transactions are routed through a conforming house that is set up under low tax jurisdiction, often with the additional benefit of double tax treaty relief.

Offshore havens are also popular areas for self-financing by finance corporations. International legislation is showing an increasing tendency to restrict relief for interest paid in companies where the high-tax authority concerned feels that inter-group loan finance is a substitute for 'proper' equity funding (for example, debt/equity ratio comparisons in the USA). Utilizing an offshore financing corporation properly makes it possible to expand greatly the allowable interest declaration.

As an alternative scheme, there is the system of 'back-to-back' financing. This system operates by routing funds through an offshore centre, thereby allowing a deposit from a low- or zero-tax jurisdiction to be linked with a corresponding borrowing from an institution in a high-tax area. The consequence will be the creation of a claim for tax relief for any interest paid, and the effect will be legally to transfer profits into a low- or zero-tax jurisdiction.

The popularity of offshore tax companies, banks, trusts and other institutions has grown tremendously in recent years. Their geographic spread is vast and ranges from the Channel Islands and the Isle of Man to Liberia, Panama, the Dutch Antilles, the British Virgin Islands, Western Samoa, Vanuatu, Luxembourg, Liechtenstein, and the states of Wyoming and Delaware in the USA. Perhaps the best-known areas at the moment are Liechtenstein and the Cayman Islands owing to the on-going scandals involving the missing Maxwell pension funds and the Bank of Credit and Commerce International (BCCI). Different areas demand different standards of disclosure, and in-depth research is needed to choose the area that best suits your objectives.

Of course, many people use offshore tax companies for perfectly honourable and legitimate reasons, but they are also popular for 'flight capital', 'keep-quiet cash', and the proceeds of classic fraud. In the recent BCCI scandal, the Luxembourg-based bank had links with the following Cayman Island-registered concerns:

1 ICIC (Overseas), which was a shadow company of BCCI and lent money against shares in BCCI (Luxembourg) and made loans to shareholders to enable them to hold on to their shares or to indemnify them against losses.

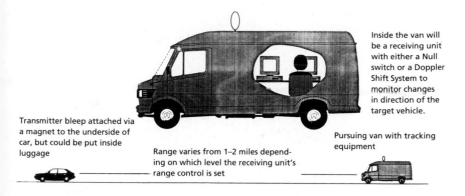

Inside the van will be a receiving unit with either a Null switch or a Doppler Shift System to monitor changes in direction of the target vehicle.

Transmitter bleep attached via a magnet to the underside of car, but could be put inside luggage

Range varies from 1–2 miles depending on which level the receiving unit's range control is set

Pursuing van with tracking equipment

ABOVE: A demonstration of a Vehicle Tracking System/Homer in action.

BELOW: Example of a surveillance vehicle using optical and audio listening devices.

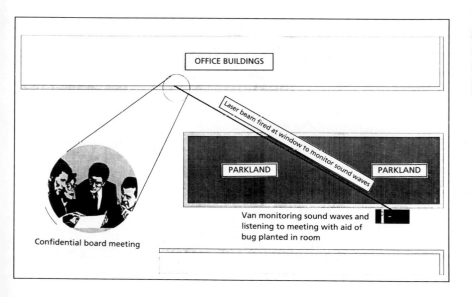

OFFICE BUILDINGS

Laser beam fired at window to monitor sound waves

PARKLAND

PARKLAND

Van monitoring sound waves and listening to meeting with aid of bug planted in room

Confidential board meeting

A metal-body cigarette packet camera, developed for the US Signal Corps *circa* 1949–50. The camera fitted into the actual outer wrapper from a Lucky Strike cigarette packet and could make eighteen exposures on 16mm film.

A very rare matchbox camera made in Germany *circa* 1938, embellished with a Nazi eagle on its underside.

This matchbox camera is also of German origin. The action of pushing the camera forward inside the matchbox opened the front flap and released the shutter, which was then reset on the reverse action.

A Minox camera with 15mm lens, made in Latvia. It dates from the German occupation of the Baltic states before the advancing Red Army occupied Latvia. Note the Nazi eagle insignia engraved on the front plate.

[Photographs courtesy of Christie's, South Kensington, London]

LEFT: A 3.5 x 5mm chrome-metal body ring camera, with a 10mm lens.

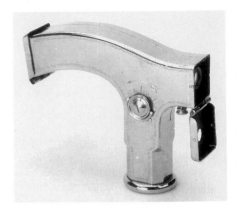

RIGHT: A replica Ben Akiba walking stick camera with five internally contained film spools. The design was patented by Emile Kronke in 1902.

BELOW: A modern wristwatch camera outfit. The quartz digital watch has an integral 5.63mm lens.

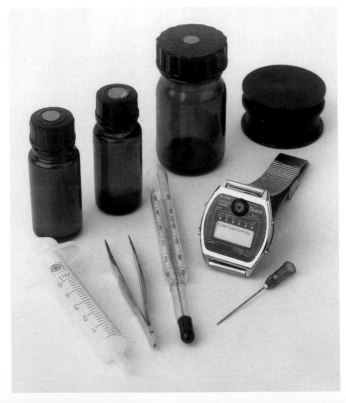

[Photographs courtesy of Christie's, South Kensington, London]

The Robot SC-electronic 33mm camera can be incorporated into various camouflage cases, as shown here. *[Robot Foto and Electronic, Dusseldorf]*

This 35mm document copying camera was made by the Russian KGB and was used by the KGB and the East German Stasi secret police during the 1950s. *[Courtesy of Christie's, South Kensington, London]*

A complete portable reprographic unit can now be housed in a lightweight attaché case, which will operate independently from the mains supply or prevailing light conditions. *[Robot Foto and Electronic, Dusseldorf]*

This night vision system provides long range observation both day and night by amplifying naturally occuring residual light, diffused light, moonlight or starlight. *[Spycatcher, London]*

One of the smallest tape recording systems available, with maximized sensitivity to the human voice. Ideal for business meetings, financial transactions, interviews and covert intelligence gathering. *[Spycatcher, London]*

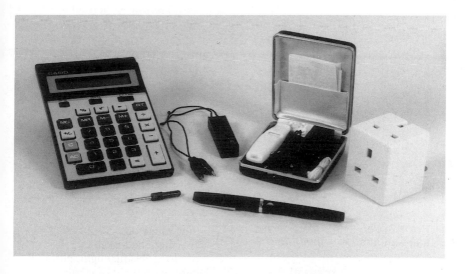

Transmitters are available in many guises, including this fully functional calculator and pen. The infinity transmitter on the right utilizes the telephone line to transmit a room's conversation to anywhere in the world. *[Spycatcher, London]*

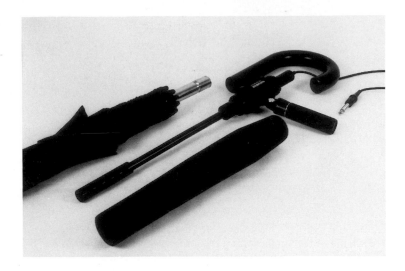

An example of a directional microphone which can be adapted for use in an 'ordinary' umbrella. *[Spycatcher, London]*

Beware the corporate free gift. Only the cassette – which has been added to provide perspective – does not contain an electronic eaves-dropping device. *[Spycatcher, London]*

2 BCCI (Overseas), which was a hundred per cent owned by BCCI Holdings in Luxembourg.

3 ICIC Foundation, a UK charity based in Cayman which owned thirty-five per cent of the Banque de Commerce et Placements in Geneva.

4 ICIC Staff Benefit Trust in Cayman.

5 ICIC Staff Benefit Fund in Cayman

as well as a link with Credit and Commerce American Holdings – a shell company established in the summer of 1978 in the largely unregulated Dutch Antilles.

Within the debacle that became the BCCI scandal, a complex system of offshore shell companies wrought havoc with international regulations and banking conformism. By using several offshore entities – BCCI in the Cayman Islands, BCCI in Luxembourg, and ICIC – these shell companies were able to lend money to one another and thus capitalize each other. A loan would be created one morning and a shareholder would find himself having just borrowed considerable sums of money. The appropriate documentation would follow identifying the shareholder, together with a loan on which neither the principal nor the interest would have to be paid back because the lender would simply increase the amount of the loan as the interest increased and promise to indemnify the shareholder by means of a 'hold harmless letter'. As a result the transaction lacked substance and became an exercise in high-flying paper.[2] BCCI is, one hopes, an extreme example of what goes on day in and day out, but how can one check before the collapse occurs? With such an obsessive emphasis on secrecy, how can one broach those confidential walls to gain sight of client assets? The answer greatly depends on where one is looking, as the myriad offshore havens have varying standards of disclosure as well as a flexible attitude towards confidentiality. The consequences of being caught 'in flagrante' while extracting information marked secret have taught many a miscreant a salutary lesson.

The key factor to remember is the 'false flag' or 'sting'

operation whereby the corporate intelligence representative will already have done a great deal of pro-active research by means of the sources discussed earlier. The intelligence analyst will already have completed a draft report and will probably have a good idea that Mr X or company Y is behind an offshore entity. By making enquiries through company research agents or directly with the appropriate Companies House in the chosen offshore haven, he will have details of nominees with names, addresses and, in some cases, telephone and fax numbers. Where the latter are not provided, international directory enquiries are normally very obliging.

At this juncture he should either delegate to an enquiry agent well versed in the art of the 'false flag' or 'sting' operation and await results, or make up his own pretext for calling. To do this he should have a good cover-story complete with name, company name, address, fax and telephone numbers. Generally, a confident and authoritative tone of voice will produce the desired result from a hassled nominee's assistant in the office at the other end. A time-honoured pretext for calling is to 'pose' as an international bank desirous of wire-transferring £n from X account to the account of Mr A of company B at such and such an address. Even where the account number is not given voluntarily, the nominees are normally more than happy to receive a cheque and will pay it in to the client's account immediately. The next step is to wait for your cheque to be cashed and clear the system. Then notify your bank to send you the cheque once it has been returned. On the back of the cheque you will find the details of the account and bank to which the funds have been transferred. It won't of course tell you how much is in the account, but at least a start has been made in asset-tracing.

CHAPTER EIGHT

Preventative Medicine

Stop up the access and passage to remorse
William Shakespeare[1]

So far this work has concentrated on the role of the hunter
and not the hunted, but what if you as an individual, or one
of your corporations, feels under threat from either an enemy
within, an enemy without, or both? The most appropriate solution to this problem is preventative medicine, and this can
best be achieved by a combination of the risk audit and escape
and evasion techniques.

THE RISK AUDIT

1 Identify the sensitive areas within the company.
2 Identify the company's secrets.
3 Were all employees vetted thoroughly?
4 Are all staff reviews up to date?
5 What are your long- and short-term forecasts for the company's prospects?
6 Is there a threat? If so, who are the likely players; how well
do you know them; what allies and resources do they have?
7 Identify what protective measures you might have available
to you, such as access control, a divide and rule policy,
banning personal laptop computers and mobile photocopiers on the premises, strict supervision of visits and waste
disposals, video scanners, computer and CCTV surveillance,

strict confidentiality agreements, avoiding the provision of product literature, keeping your company private, and making the minimum necessary disclosure requirements.

8 Anticipate losses in a doomsday scenario such as arson or sabotage; have a PR company make contingency plans; consult insurers; liaise with local police; reduce insurance premiums by contracting in a security company; assess and analyse costs of prevention.

9 Construct a security strategy in terms of effectiveness and time and budget forecasting.

COMPUTER-ASSISTED RISK ANALYSIS

An increasingly popular method of assessing risks is to use computer software specifically designed to help close gaps in security. While some of the larger multinationals employ management consultancy firms specifically to assess the security threat, this system can be expensive. There are now computer programmes that will perform an 'off the shelf' risk analysis check. One such scheme is called CRAMM – the CCTA Risk Analysis and Management Method. CRAMM evolved as a result of a study initiated in 1985 by the Central Computer and Telecommunications Agency to explore constructive methods by which central governmental departments could process unclassified but sensitive data. The system absorbs data relating to an institution's assets, the known or perceived threats to the organization, and its vulnerabilities. These three criteria are then broken down into risks and appropriate counter-measures are designed to tackle the problems. This process can be described as risk analysis or risk management. The system is now available to both the public and the private sectors, and full details can be obtained from HM Treasury.

ESCAPE AND EVASION TECHNIQUES
1 Individuals

1 Avoid the press but do not become so paranoid that you will attract attention to yourself. The obsessive secrecy of the Reichmann brothers of Olympia and York fame had become the focus of media attention long before their Canary Wharf development floundered.

2 Avoid large anonymous donations that will arouse speculation and comment.

3 Live abroad – this can also be useful for tax reasons.

4 Use offshore companies where disclosure is minimal.

5 If the formation of a UK company is really necessary, make the minimal disclosure requirements necessary.

6 Avoid making your company public. Where you need to raise money do so by mortgages or loans and not equity.

7 Use a complex system of companies to control your organization. Use 'shell' or non-active companies.

8 Wherever possible use nominees for directors or shareholders. Queen Elizabeth II uses Bank of England nominees.

9 Divide your company among different areas of the world.

10 Do not mark premises or vehicles.

11 Live modestly.

12 Avoid high-profile areas such as auction houses, nightclubs and racetracks.

13 Register your telephone as ex-directory and in a different name.

14 Pay all bills in cash and ensure that gas, electricity, water bills as well as the council tax are registered in different names.

15 As the community charge or 'poll tax' is based on the voters roll, excessive secrecy could cause complications, so consider registering to vote under a different name. Professional advice should be taken as to the exact legality of

this point. If legality is a problem and you still want discretion, it is better not to vote at all.

16 Never give interviews.

17 Avoid relationships with high-profile people.

18 Encourage all members of your family to do the same.

19 Avoid callers, especially well-dressed people with business cards and educated accents.

20 Monitor unavoidable callers, especially if they ask to use your telephone.

21 If suspicious for any reason, always obtain descriptions of people and vehicles.

22 Ensure that your house has adequate security measures such as mortise locks and infra-red detectors.

23 Paint a thin layer of clear nail varnish on key areas of your telephone; this will form a basic tamper-proof invisible seal.

24 To check whether your phone has been tampered with, use the following basic test. Go to the telephone junction box nearest your house. Check the angle and depth of the screws and the screw-heads. Photograph the scene and then leave the screws not fully tightened. Often people interfering with a junction box will tighten all screws when leaving.

25 Leave 'tell-tales' around the secured area. An example would be a piece of hair over a door or a window.

26 Use a Polaroid instant camera to ensure that your memory of the secured area does not fail you.

27 Take care with rubbish disposal.

2 Companies

1 Use a complex corporate structure.

2 Consider using offshore companies to reduce disclosure requirements as well as taking advantage of tax-avoidance schemes.

3 Change the structure of the company occasionally to make

it difficult for outsiders to gather accurate intelligence.

4 Avoid meeting the press, but where absolutely necessary use a well-briefed spokesman.
5 Change the year-ends occasionally so that comparisons with previous years' accounts are harder to make.
6 Ensure that the company has as many different share classes as possible.
7 Arrange for your master company, if it is a quoted company, to be transformed into what is ostensibly an investment operation and ensure that the actual operating companies remain private to take advantage of lower disclosure requirements.
8 Do not mark premises or vehicles with company logo or name.
9 Avoid making your company public in which case the disclosure requirements are more onerous. Where money is the issue, try to raise it through mortgages or loans and not share issues.
10 Introduce access control.
11 Vet all staff thoroughly.
12 Consider performing regular electronic sweeps.
13 Use a system of zoned colour-coding for all staff and visitors.
14 Draft authoritative and comprehensive codes of conduct.
15 Monitor all staff and visitors.
16 Check all new technology that enters the office for bugs.
17 Always use cross-cut shredders.
18 Take care with waste disposal.
19 When not needed, localize and cut out power supply.
20 Educate employees in security awareness.

3 Products

1 Alter the product by name and shape even if the innovation is small.
2 Patent the product.

3 If not patentable, file misleading claims. This can throw the opposition off the scent.

4 Pursue litigation as often as possible as a deterrent.

5 Monitor waste disposal.

6 Avoid using standard shapes for transporting goods.

7 Introduce access control methods and visible identification tags for all employees on the shop floor.

HOW TO AVOID 'LEAKS' IN YOUR COMPANY

To ensure that information does not go astray you should apply the following criteria, which will fit most scenarios. Of course, no situation is ever exactly the same, and the most appropriate standard for any security audit will depend very much on the circumstances in each individual case.

1 Conduct thorough CV checks as part of a due-diligence enquiry before all new employees are recruited.

2 Conduct a discreet review of existing employees to ensure that correct procedures were followed at all stages of recruitment. Where this was not done, recheck all records.

3 Seal off security-sensitive areas – grant access only to key employees and impose human or electronic access at terminals and key operational centres.

4 Employ a clean-desk-and-locked-drawer policy.

5 Review all staff reviews. Are there any areas of concern that might render the employee a volunteer agent or a victim of blackmail? Analyse political preferences – if the industry is scientific or industrial, do any employees show sympathy towards ecological parties or even animal rights groups?

6 Use cross-cut shredders wherever possible and avoid single-slice shredders. The most public case of reconstitution from single-slice shredders is well documented in

the story of the Iranian government recovering a wealth of 'destroyed' confidential waste shredded by US embassy officials when they abandoned their embassy in Tehran in 1990.[2] One of the biggest problems is that slices of paper are cut together and thus fall together in piles, and when the paper is of differing colours or motifs then the task of reconstituting these 'jigsaws' is made considerably easier.

7 When disposing of waste, ensure that it really is the council who is collecting your rubbish. If need be, consider employing contractors to collect and destroy your waste. Better still, never throw anything critical or sensitive away, and only dispose of 'plants' that might mislead the opposition.

8 Be wary of false-flag or 'sting' operations by mail, telephone or by a physical approach. These may involve any number of methods, including fake CVs for job applications. To avoid granting access, use strict entry procedures whereby all approaches do not get beyond the reception area. Ensure that those visitors who are granted access are never left alone. If someone needs to visit the bathroom, stand outside the door to ensure that they do not get 'lost'. It is astonishing how easy it is to win a person's confidence by using guile. One of my earlier jobs provided old leather briefcases for all employees. As I was going for my interview, I happened to be carrying a similarly styled briefcase which I had been given by my grandparents for school. That obvious familiarity of product and my jovial manner helped me pass through the whole security network unchecked. I even identified the correct office on the correct floor without being challenged by anyone. The Head of Personnel was both impressed and at the same time horrified, but it certainly helped me to 'sell' my services and I was awarded the job. I don't know what happened to the security guard.

9 Where suspicions are aroused, consider employing an outside firm to apply electronic counter-measures to 'sweep' your offices for listening devices or bugs, and also to install

a listening device on certain key lines where employee dishonesty is suspected.

10 Monitor the photocopier numbering system to check for misuse. In addition, use a timer system to monitor when the machine is in use. Better still, deny access to the photocopier to all but key personnel and only at certain times of the day. Aside from the loss of possibly crucial company information, the illegal use of the photocopier could constitute a breach of Section 11 of the Theft Act (1968), which concerns the misappropriation of electricity, and a breach of Section 1 of the Act as regards photocopying paper. Some companies might want to consider employing special paper on which to print their confidential material, which will leave an identifying mark when photocopied. All of the above presupposes the existence of company photocopiers in place and ready for misuse, but what of mobile photocopiers? The best solution is to ensure that all bags are thoroughly checked by security personnel on entry.

11 What of visitors to the office who are invitees and perhaps carry covert cameras or tape recorders in their briefcases? It is not possible to ask them to open their cases and to request that they leave them in another room might be undiplomatic – they need to preserve their own security as well. The better but more expensive solution is to install an electromagnetic or X-ray force field in the doorway or corridor through which they must pass. Any camera film or audio tape inside the case will normally either be wiped clean or its quality will be severely impaired.

12 Use codes in correspondence to hide the true name of the subject or product specifications.

13 Be economical when communicating on the telephone.

14 Use blinds or net curtains on windows to counter outside penetration.

15 Know your neighbours, especially in a multi-tenanted office block.

16 In the words of the old Allied propaganda message, 'Walls have ears', so watch what you say anywhere.

CHAPTER NINE

Walls Have Ears: Electronic Eavesdropping

Go right on and listen as thou goest
Dante[1]

The expression 'walls have ears' comes from an Allied World War II propaganda poster referring to the threat of Nazi spies overhearing information on Allied war plans. Even in those days the threat of eavesdropping existed. Nowadays, with no defined enemy, no official declaration of war, the apparent sterility of the law, and vastly more sophisticated systems available, the threat is far greater.

On 28 October 1986, Woolworth Holdings, the retailing group, realized that their phones had been tapped. A bug was discovered connected to the telephone line outside the home in Aspley Heath, Bedfordshire of Peter Hopper, a buying director of Comet, a Woolworth subsidiary. The device was crude and consisted of a small cassette recorder buried in a biscuit tin and covered in a plastic bag. The machine was linked to the telephone line by a cable and had a small automatic start-stop mechanism to record incoming and outgoing calls. As a result of the bag's discovery, three men were convicted for conspiring to intercept a telephone line.[2]

Of course, some telephone tapping is both legal and necessary, even in our democratic society. Such telephone tapping must be authorized by the Home Secretary, and a warrant will normally be granted when there is a suggestion of subversion or terrorism. The taps are carried out at the telephone exchange and are totally undetectable. According to articles in the *Guardian* newspaper, approximately thirty-five thousand taps per annum are carried out by seventy specialist BT engineers known as 'secret squirrels'.[3] In 1990 there were 539 disclosed warrants issued. However, in the field of corporate intelligence-gathering there are few who could plead state security as a valid excuse for state intervention, or indeed who are that well connected to the Home Secretary.

The media are becoming increasingly aware of corporate spying by electronic eavesdropping, yet few people are ever caught. This is because of the nature of the game, which employs people from discreet backgrounds, the fact that the law is woefully inadequate, and because discovery is too often too late, the culprits and their equipment having fled.

THE LAW

The United Kingdom law on eavesdropping is a travesty of justice and a mass of contradictions. The current law is out-dated and has failed to keep pace with advances in modern technology and the rampages of the press in their quest for information 'in the public interest'. The recent press revelations regarding 'Squidgygate', 'Camillagate' and the David Mellor scandal show that drastic solutions are needed to protect an individual's privacy. The Calcutt Report's recommendations[4] are encouraging, and it is likely that some sort of privacy legislation will be on the statute books by the mid 1990s. But what of the law as it now stands?

In 1360 advice was given to local Justices that: 'Such as listen under walls or windows, or in the eaves of a house, to hear news and carry it to others to make strife and debate amongst their neighbours, or thereupon to frame slanderous and mischievous tales, are a common nuisance, and can be bound over by the magistrates to be of good behaviour.'[5] This advice was noted in a 1982 case in the Staffordshire magistrates court. A Mr Jones had secretly installed a microphone in the ceiling of his next-door neighbour's bedroom and had listened to his neighbours' love-making for three years. According to a police lawyer: 'The case was dealt with as a breach of the peace under a Middle Ages law because technically there is no offence of eavesdropping.'[6] This case demonstrates that in the United Kingdom we have only an archaic law of limited use because it is designed to deal with minor offences. The sleazy side of the case was echoed in David Mellor's liaison with the actress Antonia de Sancha, when their privacy was invaded by an eavesdropper using his own listening equipment in an adjacent flat.

Other relevant UK statutes include the Wireless Telegraphy Act of 1949, which gives a maximum fine of £2000 where the bug is a radio transmitter that sends its signal on an unauthorized frequency and is used in a way that could interfere with a radio channel. Where the extraction of electricity is involved, an offence may be committed by breach of Section 11 of the Theft Act (1968) which concerns the unauthorized use of electricity. A possible offence may also be committed by breach of the Criminal Damage Act (1971). Some progress has been made by the Interception of Communications Act (1985) which makes it an offence to interfere with telephone lines, but this does not extend to room bugs and so would appear to exclude the infinite device which will be discussed later in this chapter. An alternative remedy for claiming damages may lie in the civil courts, though such actions can be slow and victims will need patience, determination and a healthy bank balance to contest a civil case. Another problem with the UK courts is that, even where the victim's claim is successful, there is no legal concept of punitive damages, unlike the situation in the USA, and therefore the victim must be able to prove that he has actually lost all the damages he is claiming.

Unlike the UK, almost every other industrialized Western nation has laws that aim to prevent the sale or unjustified use of surveillance devices. In the USA, it is illegal to own, sell, use or even transport devices designed for electronic surveillance. In the UK, a scan of the weekly magazine *Exchange and Mart* and an occasional visit to shops on Tottenham Court Road will reveal the existence of all manner of bugs. The present contradictory law permits the use of a radio transmitter as a

baby-minder, but how can one differentiate legally between
this device and a classic bug? A device that automatically activates a tape recorder on your own phone will also work on
another person's phone. In the UK, 'walkie-talkies' are legal
if used on certain frequencies, and there is nothing to stop one
leaving the compress switch permanently on and the 'walkie-
talkie' hidden. In addition, the 'walkie-talkie' itself could be
adapted by adding parts to convert it into a ready-tuned transmitter and receiver. It is this laxness in the UK laws and the
effectiveness of obtaining corporate intelligence in this way
that have led to the boom in electronic espionage.

TYPES OF LISTENING DEVICE

Bugs can vary in shape, range, components, life expectancy
and overall effectiveness. They can come disguised as plugs,
pens, sugar cubes, umbrellas, belts, braces, light-switches, calculators, adaptors, or specialized directional microphone bugs,
as several of the photographs in this book demonstrate. In one
famous incident, a bug was discovered built into the American
seal on a wall in the American ambassador's office in the US
embassy in Moscow. The seal had been a gift of friendship from
the Soviets to the American people, and the bug provided useful
information on American policy for a long period. However,
many of these exotic types of listening device are not nearly as
effective as the old-fashioned line-tap, directional microphone
or infinite device. These devices will now be discussed in more
detail. Needless to say, electricity can be dangerous, and anyone
contemplating dealing with these devices should seek the advice
of professionals wherever possible.

Infinite device

This is a transmitter that uses the phone line as a conduit and
monitors the room in which the phone is situated. An infinite
device can be concealed anywhere on the target phone line

or actually inside the telephone in the room itself. The user will call the target telephone number from anywhere in the world and activate the infinite transmitter by sending a tone-signal down the line. The tone is matched to a receiving unit in the bug and is produced by a small electronic device called a tone generator or harmonic. The system is parasitic in that it lives off the power generated by the line and will only work with a direct dialling system. A switchboard system will defeat this type of bug. Infinite devices are legal in both the UK and in the USA as burglar alarms.

Hookswitch block

The hookswitch is the area on the telephone where you place the handset when the phone is not in use. By blocking the hookswitch, the telephone can become a bug. This is done by connecting a low-value resistor across it. This will allow adequate electrical current to pass and activate the microphone. The eavesdropper will use an amplifier which can easily be purchased in an electrical shop. He will use a bluff call to make contact with the target telephone and not hang up when the target does. An advantage is that the system is relatively inexpensive.

Telemonitors

These are electronic switches which are closed while the telephone is in use. Known in the trade as 'drop-out relays', they consist of a small box with a couple of wires and crocodile clips which are attached to the telephone. Their power is supplied by batteries or drawn parasitically from the mains, and they can be connected anywhere on the telephone line. Popular with businessmen, they are often used to record sensitive telephone conversations. They can easily be installed by the layman using an insertion tool or penknife to connect the wires to a tape recorder at the telephone wall-socket. Used in this way, there is no particular need for discretion.

Laser bug

This is similar to a contact bug which uses window vibrations to generate sounds. A pulsed power supply is applied to a laser and the laser beam pointed at the window. When light-waves hit the vibrating glass, they are modulated. The light is reflected back, refocussed and made to pass through a pin-hole and onto a photomultiplier tube. This tube will detect pulse variations according to width and translate them into sound. Equipment is often housed in the backs of motor vans or across the street in an adjacent building. A typical example can be found among the illustrations in this book.

Infra-red transmitter

An infra-red transmitter should be positioned by a window to maximize the effect. A special receiver is needed which must be linked to a converter and amplifier to convert the infra-red waves into audible sound — some are built into the bodies of single-lens reflex cameras. The technology required makes the system expensive and its value must therefore be doubted, considering the more effective and cheaper systems that are available. The receiver will often be housed inside a vehicle which should be parked in close proximity to the target transmitter.

Direct tapping

Direct taps are easy to apply and compared with many systems are inexpensive. Although the tap can be placed anywhere along the line, the wire-stripping and connections involved tend to cause audible clicking sounds on the line. To avoid this eavesdroppers apply the tap at the junction or terminal box. The target phone will be selected and an oscillator connected to it by wire-splicing. A device called a non-linear junction detector is then installed at the directing box or in the frame-room (in the case of large premises). This machine detects the signal being emitted by the oscillator and identifies the target line. The bug will then be applied and linked to a tape recorder concealed somewhere on the premises. The sound quality is normally excellent and the tap can often be placed on the line in a lower security area well away from the target telephone.

Radio bugs

Bug manufacturers buy standard microphones from the same sources as the telephone companies and dissect them, disposing of the carbon granules within and using the remaining space for a mini-magnetic microphone and transmitter unit. The system is parasitic with a range of up to four hundred metres. Radio bugs can be housed in a host of different objects, many of which are desk-compatible. Examples include lampshades, ashtrays and calculators.

The telephoner re-dialler (cheesebox)

This is attached to the telephone and automatically redirects any incoming calls to a pre-set number without the caller being aware of the fact. The system is used legitimately by doctors and business people offering twenty-four-hour cover. Many of the more advanced telephones and answering machines employ this technology.

The relay system

A relay can be of great use where a bug has only a short range. A receiver is linked to a powerful transmitter which will re-transmit the product of the bug to an expanded area. The relay system can be located in a vehicle or in a nearby room. The system absorbs a lot of power, so often a car battery is used, unless access to the mains is not a problem. Another disadvantage is that distance can compromise quality.

*   *   *

It is possible that the quality of the sound recorded may be poor. To obviate this, an audio compressor may be used which can assist in levelling out different sound volumes. The device is attached between the microphone and the transmitter or recorder and adjusted according to whether the listener wants to increase the softer sounds or reduce the louder ones. The frequency equalizer is a complementary system that helps to focus the key parts of the conversation by eliminating background noise.

TYPES OF MICROPHONE

The world of high technology has come a long way from the old 'mike monstrosities' that used to be endemic in the industry. However, condensed technology often brings with it increased prices which will deter all but the more serious 'snoops'. In addition, a more compact device is no guarantee of enhanced quality. It is therefore only in the more shady covert enquiries that mini-microphones will be required.

Many microphones are large-scale and have exotic names such as shotgun, machine-gun, and rifle. A shotgun microphone is a long, tube-like instruments that has a pistol grip and can measure up to three feet long. It has been known to have been built into an umbrella. It is a favourite of television companies. The machine-gun microphone consists of a series of small cups mounted in rows along a central tube. The cups act as noise traps to concentrate the sound. A rifle microphone, often seen in location television interviews, is similar to the shotgun microphone and is also designed to pick up distant sounds. A big disadvantage is the overt nature of these devices, and the fact that they also amplify background noise. Any noise so picked up can be eliminated using a frequency analyser that will allow you to magnify selected frequencies and eliminate others that are not needed, though again the cost factor should be borne in mind.

Parabolic mike

This is popular with bird-watchers who like to record bird-song. It consists of a large circular metal or plastic dish which reflects sound onto a microphone mounted in the centre. While comparatively inexpensive, it is not as sensitive as other systems and its high visibility gives the device limited application.

Contact mike

A contact microphone responds to vibrations in a 'sounding board' rather than in the air. Typical sounding boards are doors, windows or walls. The microphone will be glued or pressed against the surface and any vibrations will be picked up. Quality can vary enormously. As a rule of thumb, the thicker the surface the harder it will be to hear anything. Another downside of this system is that one may have to get too close to the target. An alternative is to use laser beams fired at a window (see above).

Small directional mike

These tend to be used over short distances. They are compact, normally discreet, and can be worn up the sleeve or disguised in a handbag, briefcase or fountain pen. They will normally be attached to a pocket-size tape recorder. One system produced by CCS is activated as soon as the pen is removed from its housing on the tape recorder. The microphone is mounted in a bell-shaped housing and is especially good for eavesdropping on restaurant or street conversations, although heavy traffic can severely impair sound quality.

Tube mike

A tube mike is a small sealed container with a microphone housed inside. A thin plastic tube protrudes from the container. One end of the tube is attached to the front of the microphone. The fact that the box is sealed ensures that the microphone will only intercept sound received through this tube. The container is connected to an amplifier and one end of the tube stuck into a keyhole, under a door, or through a small hole drilled in a wall. These systems are particularly popular in hotels, which invariably have back-to-back sockets and switches.

Spike mike

One of the failings of the aforementioned contact mike is the problem with surface thickness, which can severely impair sound quality. One way to obviate this problem is to use a spike mike which is, as the name suggests, a spike attached to a microphone which is hammered or drilled into the wall. As the spike nears the extremity of the inner target wall, it will pick up sound vibrations and transmit them back into the listening room.

Body mike

Typical examples are built into tie-clips, belts, braces, wrist-watches, cuff-links, buttons and pens. Invariably they will be attached to small pocket-size recorders, such as the Olympus Pearlcorder. When using such a microphone to maintain contact with your surveillance team, it is important not to angle your mouth towards the microphone when speaking. This is not simply for reasons of discretion but also because the microphone is designed to absorb your speech from a certain distance. It is extraordinary how self-conscious some novices are when first using such equipment.

VOX – Voice-activated switch

Many systems possess VOX which not only preserves battery life but also saves on valuable audio-tape and transcription time. A VOX switch will be connected to the power circuit between the transmitter and its battery. The switches use a pre-set level and once sound is detected at the set level the switch will close, allowing the transmitter to operate. Once the sound level falls beneath the chosen level the switch re-opens. There is a built-in delay to avoid the switch opening and closing every time there is a slight pause in the conversation.

TELEVISION BUGS

Television has now entered the bugging arena through the use of fibre-optics. As a result, both voices and pictures can now be transmitted and received. Television signals can be detected more easily than simple voice signals as they use a greater band width than radio signals. You will need a receiver, a camera and a lens with a TV transmitter and aerial. The advantage of fibre-optics is that the lens need not be in the same place as the camera, and it can therefore be placed in pin-holes drilled through walls, built into lights, and even hung down chimneys.

WIRELESS LANS

A LAN is a local area network. Many computer systems used in commerce and industry are linked by personal computers to LANs. It is becoming increasingly popular to use radios instead of land lines to communicate along these LANs. In the UK, the microwave band of 2.412–2.438 GHz is used, while in the USA the equivalent systems use 902–925 MHz. To eavesdrop on a radio LAN, you should simply install a receiver in any area close to the target. Although equipment costs can be high, the system does have its advantages over more conventional methods – for example, the fact that wireless LANs use 'spread spectrum techniques' whereby all the 'channels' use the entire length of the frequency band available and band usage is constantly being changed to optimize the benefit of the available resources. The 'spread spectrum' system is also used for high-security voice traffic.

FAX/TELEX TAPS

It is a popular misconception that only a telephone can be tapped. When a fax is transmitted, the calling and receiving fax machines are intertwined in a constant 'call and response cycle' to prevent errors. Thus, a fax intercept must be able to hold back the reception of certain signals while recording the remainder. The interceptor will need a fax modem and a knowledge of the special diagnostic codes used by the victim fax machine.

The telex is the oldest form of digital data transmission. Telexes are preferable to telephone transmissions for the interceptor as they rely on digital transmissions which often avoid a lot of the irrelevancies that arise in a normal telephone conversation. Nowadays telex facilities are available on cards that can be inserted into personal computers and doctored for the purposes of interception.

HOMING DEVICES

These are technically not bugs but beacons, and can be used as either an audible bleep or as a silent infra-red flash that is invisible to the naked eye. They achieved notoriety in the film *Goldfinger* when James Bond attached one to the rear underside of Aurel Goldfinger's vintage Rolls-Royce at his golf club. Once the device was activated, Bond was able to follow the signal across Europe in his Aston Martin using a detailed electronic map. Such sophisticated devices do not exist in reality, but more rudimentary models are available.

Technically speaking a 'homer' comprises a transmitter unit that produces a series of high-powered electronic pulses and

a receiving unit or monitor that listens for the signal and inter-
prets it as a series of beeps. Normally, it will come with small
magnets with which to attach the device beneath a vehicle. A
'homer' can be of any size but increasingly they are of a compact variety. Typically, it will consist of extremely thin
components with a strand of wire as an antenna. It can be
laminated onto a business card and is parasitic in that it
acquires power through radiation given off by other electrical
devices. A popular beacon used to locate stolen vehicles in the
USA is 'Lojack', which has been successfully tested by the West
Midlands Constabulary and looks set to be introduced into the
UK on a commercial basis in the near future.

There are three types of receivers. Firstly, the antenna,
which is rudimentary, possesses no direction-finding capability, and relies solely on volume to indicate the source of
the transmitter. Secondly, there are directional receivers that
consist of either a vertically mounted looped aerial attached
to the pursuing vehicle or, alternatively, a matching pair of
aerials – one placed on each side of the tail vehicle. As soon
as the signal is located, you should reposition the vehicle and
aerial until the signal reaches its optimum strength. As you
get closer to your target you will hear the signals merge into
a single continuous sound. Thirdly, there is a range-control
facility, which normally provides three positions ranging from
short distances (one to two miles) to long distances (five to six
miles) and is useful when trying to avoid getting too close to
the target vehicle. An example is illustrated. Another method
of avoiding close proximity to your prey is by using the Null
switch. Once this switch is selected, the receiver will remain
silent if your target is directly in front or behind you. However,
if your target moves right or left then a different sound will
be heard, depending on which way the vehicle has turned. It
is particularly useful on main roads.[7]

A typical escape and evasion technique is for the target
vehicle to perform a U-turn and turn back on itself. To counter
this threat, the industrial spy should employ a system known
as a 'Doppler shift' which can warn the person following of

the target doing a U-turn.[8] A 'Doppler shift' system works by measuring the radio waves that emanate from a moving object. These waves will increase in wavelength if the object is moving away and shorten when it is moving closer. Thus, when the system shows a zero reading, it means that both hunter and quarry are travelling at the same speed. When positive, it will indicate the speed at which your target is moving away from you. When negative, the target will either have slowed down or will have turned and be heading away from you. Doppler electronics are often used in airborne military radar systems and are very expensive.

ANSWERPHONES

Fast becoming a standard feature in most households, many of the more technically advanced models have remote facilities that enable the owners to hear their messages without the hassle of returning to base. To achieve this play-back feature, these models use a touch-tone system or, for pulse-generated systems, a separate tone pad. The plan should be to intercept the code so that you can listen to your competitor's messages. This is not as difficult as it may seem and the following principles should be followed:

(a) Establish the make of the answerphone and get an instruction book which can easily be obtained from the manufacturers.

(b) Try and gain sight of the machine as invariably the code is actually written on the appliance itself.

(c) Otherwise, use trial and error to break the code – many answerphones will respond after a two-digit code.

(d) Use a modem and computer and write a short programme to dial the number, apply a tone-mode through the modem if there is not one already, and instruct the modem to use a random selection process to establish the code.

(e) Buy a credit-card-sized pocket autodialler which will generate the appropriate tones to save you the labour of
keying them in each time. Normally, the zero prefix can
be ignored.

RADIO EAVESDROPPING

The first step in your corporate intelligence quest should be to
find out whether the company or individual you are interested
in uses radio-based services to any extent. If so, then it may
well be worth your while to consider eavesdropping, though
beware of the consequences of breaching the UK Wireless
Telegraphy Act (1949), the USA's Electronic Communications
Privacy Act (1986) or comparable legal restrictions in other
countries. The newer-version scanning radios are controlled
via a keypad similar to a calculator and combine digital control
with a radio circuit called a frequency analyser. The digital
control aspect ensures that frequencies can be memorized and
placed in memory banks that can be sampled, and that upper
and lower frequency bands can be searched. The search programme will pause when it identifies a signal before moving
on.

In the UK it is not illegal *per se* to possess a scanner, but it
is illegal to listen in, especially to the police and army, although
there does not appear to be a problem with radio enthusiasts
listening to commercial aircraft transmissions. The problem lies
not in the theory but in the practice of enforceability – it is
very difficult to get caught. In Germany and Finland the law
is far stricter and it is a criminal offence to possess a scanner.
The attempts of James Cran MP to introduce a Control of
Electronic Surveillance Devices Bill in the UK in May 1989
failed.[9] It is to be hoped that the recent media activity with
respect to the Royal Family will lead to a more robust law of
privacy after the matter is debated in the House of Commons
during 1994.

Many more traditional sorts of mobile radio applications

operate on fixed frequencies, such as those used by the police, fire and ambulance services. In addition, CB radio operates on a fixed-frequency service with up to forty channels from which to choose. Thus, once found, the target will always be there. According to an article in the *Sunday Telegraph*, the police are considering using message scramblers to ensure privacy.

A radio wave system operates along the radio frequency spectrum, and its use is determined first by international agreement through the International Telecommunications Union and various World Administrative Radio Conferences, and secondly by national practice. A third method is a network of publications circulated unofficially among radio enthusiasts. The radio spectrum is a crowded place with each single megahertz of the spectrum holding up to eighty separate radio channels, each of which has the capability of distinctive usage.

CORDLESS PHONES

These use only a few channels and in the UK concentrate on three sets of radio frequencies, namely 49 MHz, 47 MHz and 1900 KHz, while the USA uses 49 MHz and 46 MHz. Their range is only 100–200 metres, and so any attempt at interception should take place close to the base station. Once you have 'locked on' to the target, you should set up a tape recorder ready to be activated as soon as your radio picks something up. A system of cordless phones that grew up in the late 1980s and was pioneered in the UK was that of base-station phones, such as the Zone phone. They relied on reception points being dotted around towns, but were not popular and are now almost redundant.

CELLULAR PHONES

It is ironic that those business people who so zealously guard their company documents have so little awareness of the risks of compromising themselves when speaking on cellular phones. Cellular phones are big business and their use is becoming the norm in commercial circles. This usage has broadened beyond simple telephone calls as they are now also used for data and facsimile calls. A recent well-publicized example of cellular phone interception occurred in November 1990, when Richard Needham, a junior government minister in the Northern Ireland office, was driving around South Armagh and had a conversation with his wife in which he spoke in very unflattering terms about Mrs Thatcher. The IRA intercepted the call, recorded it, and sent a copy to the press.[10] Thankfully state security secrets were not involved in this interception, but it does stress the need for caution when using this type of communication.

In spite of what may have been implied in recent press coverage of the private lives of the Royals, cellular phones are not as easy to intercept as cordless phones, as cellular radio is able to support a huge number of clients because the frequencies allocated to it are always being reused. As soon as the signal strength of a channel currently in use drops, the machine will immediately scan the area for another control channel with a stronger signal. Once found, the conversation taking place will be switched to a new pair of frequencies. The fact that the calls are constantly being switched from cell to cell gives the user a false sense of security. Just as your cellular phone can 'duck and dive' between cells, so can it be followed by good-quality scanners. High technology means that all these calls can easily be intercepted, and such phones should not be used for any sensitive traffic.

A recent survey by the Bell Telephone Company of Canada has shown that 'snoopers listen to up to 80% of calls on mobile phones and about 60% may be taped'. The press has been full of the details of the 'Squidgy' tapes allegedly revealing a passionate conversation between the Princess of Wales and James Gilbey, and the more recent revelations of 'Camillagate', representing a supposed conversation between Camilla Parker-Bowles and the Prince of Wales. These revelations regarding the Royal Family will, it is to be hoped, ensure greater vigilance on the part of those using cellular telephones.[11]

While it remains a moot point whether or not members of the Royal Family were bugged by the Intelligence Services using land-line taps, who then transmitted the information across the airwaves to be intercepted by radio hams – conduct apparently justified by reference to the Duchess of York's behaviour prior to the 1989 Iraqi invasion of Kuwait when arrangements were made for her Texan 'financial adviser' to use an office in Buckingham Palace in which to meet an Iraqi oil minister – this version of events does not dilute the risks associated with using mobile phones.

To explain this inherent insecurity in cellular phones, one must first examine how a typical cellular radio network operates, and I have chosen as an example the TACS system. Cellular radio is a system based on cells that range in length from two kilometres in cities to up to thirty kilometres in the shires. Each of these cells will have its own base transmitter operating on several independent radio channels. These base transmitters will be linked to a central electronic network, which provides a link-up with the public switched telephone network (PSTN). The TACS system has a bi-directional signalling facility between the base station and the mobile units. The system transmits data along four separate data trails:

(a) Forward Voice Channel (FVC), which represents bursts of data transmissions on the voice channel and is used to shift channels, alternate power supply, or to end a call.

(b) Forward Control Channel (FOCC), which can be defined as a continuous data stream used primarily in the call set-up procedure. It lets the controller know the status of the reverse control channel and provides information on whether or not the phone is on the hook.

(c) Reverse Control Channel (RCC). This is similar to the FOCC but will be transmitted by the mobile system at the call set-up point. Information sent will include the electronic serial number (ESN) and appropriate phone and identification numbers.

(d) Reverse Voice Channel (RVC), which, like the FVC, is used for call management and is transmitted by the mobile system.[12]

In addition, there are also two supervisory tones, namely, the Signalling Tone (ST) and the Supervisory Audio Tone (SAT).

All the above systems show that the fundamental weakness of the cellular phone network is that the information is publicly available to any aspiring eavesdropper.

To intercept a call on cellular radio you should start by purchasing an appropriate FM scanning receiver. This system works better in country areas where there is less traffic. In a built-up area you should consider using two scanning receivers and control them with a computerized decoder system.

R1		DATA		*R2*
Scanner		DECODER		Scanner

To apply this system you must first programme the phone number and identification code of the target system into the decoder. The first scanning receiver (R1) will then monitor the FCC in the target area. As soon as a call set-up request is made by the target, the decoder unit will activate the second scanner (R2) to the base voice channel, thereby enabling it to confirm the SAT and monitor the target's conversation. The second scanner will monitor the FVC and, when a call management instruction is received, the decoder will instruct the first scanner to follow the target to the new channel and continue to eavesdrop.[13] An added bonus is that it may be possible to determine the approximate location of the target once the correct call is identified, as cell locations, SATs and frequencies can be located by analysing the trade promotional literature available and by constant monitoring. In this respect the scanners can operate like a quasi-homing system. The obvious downside to this system is the cost and the need for professional help. Few of the more prominent private security firms would publicly consent to be involved with such a system, though many of them might know someone who would help.

CHAPTER TEN

Electronic Eavesdropping – Counter-Measures

Be sober, be vigilant; because your adversary . . .
walketh about, seeking whom he may devour
St Peter[1]

Corporate intelligence-gathering is a double-edged knife –
there is always a perpetrator and always a victim. Often companies are hypocritical in that they criticize others for the very
practices they are following themselves. The previous chapter
dealt with the threat of electronic eavesdropping. This chapter
will concentrate not only on countering the threat by physical
and electronic means, but also on how you can feed false
information through electronic devices to compromise your
competitors. This can be worth considerably more than the bad
publicity generated when the perpetrators are caught. Much of
the equipment that will now be discussed is beyond the means
of the average user, and it is normally better to call in 'sweep
teams' to cleanse buildings on a regular basis. References
should always be taken up, as there are many 'cowboys' in
the field. Although they are expensive, it is often better to deal
only with the larger firms.

TELEPHONE ANALYSER

This system is used to carry out tests on telephones with a
semi-automatic facility, and is especially useful with complex
multi-line switchboards. The system is portable, expensive,
and needs a highly trained operator to carry out a series of

complex tests. The operator will first measure the voltage across the phone line when the phone is off the hook. The test analyser will then display each test result digitally to the nearest decimal point. The telephone analyser will then sweep through the audio spectrum, sending out a constantly changing tone. If there is an infinite transmitter on the line then it will be activated when the tone generator hits the right frequency. The result will be a drop in voltage which will be picked up by the analyser and will cause the tone generator to disconnect and an alarm system to be activated.

Another test method is to apply *high-voltage pulsing*, whereby the tester allows a charge to be built up in the analyser and then sent down the line. Should the handset mike be opened, the analyser will pick up the voltage to it and trigger the alarm.[2]

The final test involves *audio listening*, whereby the operator wears a pair of headphones, activates the acoustic generator and listens. If he hears a tone travelling along the line then that will indicate that some sort of hookswitch defeat is in operation.

FIELD STRENGTH METER

This is a radio set which is connected to a meter rather than a speaker. It will pick up the power output of a transmitter in the vicinity and once the target has been located will display the results by means of a swinging needle or a digital reading. Unfortunately, the system suffers from low sensitivity and a lack of discrimination – it will also pick up police transmissions.

FEEDBACK MONITORS

Feedback is the whining sound that is heard when a microphone is placed too close to an amplifier. The same effect occurs when a transmitter is taken too close to a receiver, often the case at amateurish pop concerts. To use this detector, you will need to tempt the bug to transmit by making a noise, and then scan the radio frequencies to identify the one being used by the bug.

SPECTRUM ANALYSER

As the name suggests, this device analyses the radio spectrum by sweeping the frequency bands between 20 KHz and 2000 MHz. The system will automatically scan the designated field until it 'locks on' to a transmission signal. It will then display the frequency and the signal strength on a field-strength meter, or in some cases on an oscilloscope. Much loved by radio enthusiasts, it was this system that was believed to have intercepted the 'Squidgy' conversation.

THE 'SCREAMER' CABLE-CHECKER

The 'screamer' is a small box which is attached to any convenient point along the suspect cable by baring the wires without cutting them and connecting the device using clips. Should there be a microphone on either end of the cable, it will make a loud noise once the 'screamer' is activated. A stethoscope should then be used to pinpoint the exact location of the hidden microphone.

TAP-PROOF PHONE

When the phone unit is installed it should be adjusted to alter the impedance of the phone line in such a way that whenever a call is made or received the change will be insufficient to activate a drop-out relay of a switched-line-powered bug. The system will also measure the voltage on the line and will prevent the use of hookswitch defeats and similar devices that make parasitic use of the telephone's own microphone by internally separating the telephone's functions.

COVER NOISE TO HIDE CONVERSATION

Used somewhat comically in the Tom Hanks film *The Man with One Red Shoe*, where the Head of the CIA conducts secure meetings beneath his garden sprinklers while leaving prerecorded conversations playing on his tape deck, the system is nevertheless useful. Microphones are unable to differentiate between sounds *per se*, and although frequency analysers can be used to filter out surrounding noise, these systems will be quite beyond the budget or technical competence of the average company. When using this method, it is a good idea to have a continuous sound; for example, record the background noise of a busy restaurant and amplify.

JAMMERS

Such devices are best known in totalitarian regimes for preventing the transmission or reception of unwanted messages. Many are wide-band radio transmitters that produce 'white noise' – an unintelligible and nauseous sound that renders listening impossible. As jammers tend to be very powerful, they will overpower any bugs in the vicinity, but have the added problem of interfering with your neighbour's television and radio sets. This could make you unpopular and draw attention to yourself.

An alternative jammer uses two high-frequency transmitters that transmit on different frequencies and will cause any nearby microphones to produce a high-pitched sound at the point of difference between them. The effect will be to render the bug or tape recorder quite useless.

ENCRYPTION DEVICES

Generally known as 'scramblers' and originally designed for military use, encryption devices alter the information at the transmission point by chopping the speech pattern into a few parts, mixing it up, and sending it down the line or across the airwaves, where a second unit at the receiving end converts it back into its original form. Any interception of the message en route between the two units will prove unintelligible. Although most encryption devices are portable, an operator will need two matching units and the cost can be high. It is wise to spend money on a more advanced system as simple scramblers can be intercepted.

An encryption device uses a system of speech inversion or side-band splitting to jumble up the information so that the entire frequency range of the human voice is split into a number of parts which are then mixed and transmitted. The more sophisticated scramblers rearrange the broken-down parts electronically. The order in which they are rearranged is constantly fluctuating, the system of rearrangement being controlled by a Random Code Generator (RCG). With a typical scrambler system this RCG can generate two million or more user codes, and one code will be selected on each unit by turning numbered dials secured in a locked panel. The units are then linked together by telephone, and as one person speaks a digital signal is transmitted between the units to synchronize them. Every split second the RCG will select a new code, thereby constantly jumbling the transmission. The units are kept synchronized by internal clocks.[3]

Scramblers can also be used for radio transmissions. However, a simple radio scrambler can be prone to jammers and may fall victim to direction-finding equipment. Solutions to these problems include increasing the speed of transmissions – the 'burst' system, which has been used by the SAS for a number of years – and employing a frequency hopper.

The *frequency hopper* was first introduced in 1979 for military use. It consists of an adapted VHF transmitter that allows the user to set the switches to any one of a million pre-selected codes. These codes then activate the initiating frequency and the band width over which the radio will hop. Frequency hoppers are very fast and can work over a great range. The top models can hop between up to one thousand pre-programmed frequencies over a 10-MHz spread between 650 and 750 times per minute. With the frequency changing so rapidly, direction-finding is virtually impossible.[4]

VOLTMETER TESTS

Buy a voltmeter that can read a scale of 0–75 volts DC. You should locate the junction box serving your telephone, find the two terminals connected to the main cable, and take a voltage reading. The reading should be 46–50 volts. If the reading is lower than this, it is possible that a bug has been connected in parallel. You should then lift the handset of the telephone from its cradle and re-measure the voltage, which should read between two and twelve volts. If there is a higher reading, then a bug may have been connected in series. However, it is important to note that these voltage tests will not locate a non-active infinite transmitter.

VHF-BAND RADIO/TV SET DETECTORS

Neither is an infallible system, but they represent a cost-effective method of detection and are easy enough for the novice to use. Using a VHF-band radio, you should extend the aerial, turn up the volume, and slowly turn the tuning control to scan the entire band width. If a bug is near, feedback will be generated through the speaker in your improvised 'feedback-type' detector.

Although television pictures are transmitted in UHF, the audio element utilizes VHF. You should use an ordinary aerial, make a loud noise in the area you want to check so as to activate what might otherwise remain a dormant bug, turn down the TV volume control, choose a channel, and adjust the tuning dial. If there is a VHF bug in the room, you will notice a horizontal band of white lines on the screen which will correspond with the sound volume.

THE PHYSICAL SEARCH

Always perform your search in a localized and logical fashion. It should be done in silence, preferably with background noise, floor by floor, room by room, and within each room by dividing the area into height and width zones starting at floor level. It is important not to panic or to be excessively paranoid. Admiral of the Fleet Sir Terence Lewin, GCB, MVO, DSC, Chief of the Defence Staff, tells a story about Doctor Luns, the Secretary-General of NATO, when he was Dutch Foreign Minister. Prior to his first visit to Moscow, Luns received a briefing on the dangers of electronic eavesdropping and how he should inspect his room for hidden microphones. When he reached his hotel, he searched his room thoroughly but could find neither wire nor microphone. Feeling exasperated, he scanned the walls, the ceiling and the floor. Suddenly, he noticed a lump beneath the carpet which he then lifted to reveal a wire running towards the centre of the room. Using the wire-cutters thoughtfully provided by his Intelligence Service, he cut the wire clean through and, as he rose triumphantly, he heard the sound of a loud crash from the room below as the chandelier fell from the ceiling.[5]

The following checklist is relevant in any physical search and should always be complementary to any electronic counter-measures:

(a) Search both the inside and the outside of the premises.

(b) Overhead telephone cables – follow them back to the pole.

(c) Are there any wires going into the walls – if so, do you know the reason for them?

(d) If the wires go underground, find and lift the inspection hatch.

(e) Look for wires that have been spliced into cable.

(f) Identify the telephone junction box that serves your premises. If you can open it, look inside for anything suspicious. If you find it, then call the telephone company.

(g) Inspect the window frames – are there any holes?

(h) Check the backs and bottoms of all furniture.

(i) Look under beds and on the underside of fabric.

(j) Many household objects such as lamps and ornaments have a felt base – look for signs of tampering.

(k) Check picture frames, walls, floor, ceiling, pelmets, curtains and the skirting-board.

(l) Roll back the carpets.

(m) Look for loose floorboards.

(n) Check the attic area.

(o) Are there any signs of flaked or mismatched paint anywhere?

(p) Take special care when looking at floors, walls and ceilings where the premises are part of an apartment block or a semi-detached house, as these could be used for contact or 'spike' mikes. Any holes found should be filled in.

(q) Turn off the mains supply and disconnect all fuses. Then unscrew the covers of wall sockets and light-switches and check inside.

(r) Unscrew the ceiling roses and look inside.

(s) Telephone – pick up the handset and unscrew the plastic ring holding the microphone in place. Check to see whether the alloy ring between the two halves has been cut and re-soldered. Paint nail varnish over the joints which will crack if tampered with.

(t) Check the action of the hookswitch in the telephone – ensure that it shuts off when you press it down.

(u) Use a metal detector to scan walls, floors and ceiling.

CHAPTER ELEVEN

Computer Espionage – The Threat

The summer of 1983 may prove to be the watershed period for data security. The movie *War Games*, together with the well-publicized activities of the so-called '414' gang from Milwaukee, have given more credibility to data security concerns in the eyes of the general public than a decade of hypothesizing and doomsaying by data security professionals. This may be a sad commentary on our profession, but it clearly indicates that an appeal to the emotions can be more effective than reasoned, rational argument.

Steve Gold[1]

These words amply demonstrate the frustrations felt by security professionals in educating corporations to employ adequate safeguards to protect their systems. The situation has been made more acute by the activities of the 'Michelangelo' computer virus which wrought havoc on systems around the world in early 1992.

Computer fraud is a growth industry. Donn Parker of the Stamford Research Institute has estimated damage from US computer fraud at $3000 million per annum, although actually reported crimes account for only $100 million each year. In the UK, BIS Applied Systems estimate damage from our computer frauds to be in the region of £500 million to £2500 million per year. In 1983 Detective Inspector Ken McPherson, the former head of computer crime in the Metropolitan Police, estimated that within fifteen years every fraud would involve a computer.[2] The year 1998 is not far away, and in many respects his prophecy has already been proved correct. In 1985 the Audit Commission published their 'Computer Fraud Survey' and announced that they had received 943 replies to their questionnaire of which 77 quoted instances of fraud. Of these 77 instances, 58 represented frauds carried out at the input stage, 2 represented frauds at the output stage, and 17 involved the misuse of resources by company employees.

The word hacking is often understood as being synonymous with computer fraud. However, although it is a potentially valuable aspect of corporate intelligence-gathering which can cost a company millions in insider information, hacking incidents are still relatively rare. Robert Courtney, formerly the security adviser at IBM, has said: 'The number one problem now and forever is errors and omissions. Then there is crime by insiders, particularly non-technical people of three types: single women less than 35, "little old ladies" over 50 who want to give money to charity; and older men who feel their careers have left them neglected. Next, natural disasters. Sabotage by disgruntled employees. Water damage. As for hackers and other outsiders who break in: less than 3% of the total.' Indeed, in the UK, the National Computing Centre claims that at least ninety per cent of computer crimes involve planting false information into a computer rather than more advanced techniques.

Thus, often the perpetrators of computer crime are simply employees of the victim who have the opportunity, the inside knowledge of the system, the necessary avarice, or perhaps a desire to wage a vendetta against their employers. Many will act independently for their own ends, while others may be recruited as agents to provide key access-control information. Typical examples of fraud are rounding up figures to the nearest whole number in your account, faking entries and invoices and forging input material, as well as parallel trading.

To be a successful hacker you must understand what computer systems are used by the target company and how they are used. It will assist you greatly if personal computers are widely installed, as these are seldom in high-security areas and are normally linked by network to a mainframe system, and can thus provide a gateway into far more rewarding areas. Often the most important computer system will be installed at Head Office. Once the computer system is known, obtain the appropriate reference books, which are commercially available or discussed in the numerous computer magazines. As always, there is the pretext call to your target company to be made, as well as the acquiring of trade literature from the PR department of the computer company that installed the system in the first place.

Additional intelligence starting points include making yourself aware of the internal structure of your target, as a computer system will normally reflect the target company's corporate structure. The methods described earlier in this book should be implemented.

Try to obtain a copy of an internal telephone directory, as typical passwords are often a person's initials or their first name. Consider attempting a 'false-flag' entry to the premises as, for example, a cleaner, and check for Post-it notes that bear a codeword. Try to establish the user's idiosyncrasies, such as jokes, a departmental title, the names of boyfriends or girlfriends, hobbies, favourite pop stars, football teams, interests, names of family, close friends, and bank account numbers, as all these could be potential clues as to the access code.

Try to by-pass a personal computer's access control package by using a new copy of the Disk Operating System (DOS) in the floppy disk drive and then re-booting the system. If accessing the system on the target premises, you should take with you a laptop PC – preferably with a hard disk – and employ a special file-transfer kit to shift data from the target PC to your laptop. As soon as the system is connected, the 'host' machine uses its RS232 port to communicate with the target. This method will normally by-pass any security package installed in the target PC.

Other methods to be considered include introducing a false 'sign-on-screen' to capture the passwords when used legitimately, a password try-out programme that uses trial and error to guess a valid password from variables, and a password file-decrypter programme. In using any of these methods, it should be borne in mind that you will normally need to be on the premises of the target, and unless very skilful you run the risk of leaving 'footprints' that may cause a security alert.

Another access method is to exploit the prolific use of networking along telephone lines to establish contact with your competitor's computer. This system was used with devastating effect in the aforementioned film *War Games*. You will need to have an autodialler, a utility programme, a smart modem, an RS232C port terminal, a PC, and an appropriate software package to run the call sequences through the autodialler. If possible use a fast tone dialler as the older pulse systems are considerably slower.

To obtain much of their information, hackers rely on the lackadaisical attitudes and woeful lack of security of computer salesman, programmers, operators and designers, but in spite of these lapses there is no authentic account of a UK clearing bank suffering from a large-scale pure computer fraud. This may be due partly to the banks concealing crimes so as to preserve their credibility. The classic bank fraud generally relies on a forged input form which is erroneously accepted, the computer systems then taking over.

The actual manipulation of computer files and programmes in banks is rare owing to the introduction of stringent guidelines. In the UK there is the Clearing House Automatic Payments System (CHAPS), which dates from 1984. The CHAPS system arranges for cheque-clearing and account maintenance under conditions of very tight security using the USA's Data Encryption Standard. The international equivalent of CHAPS is SWIFT, or the Society for Worldwide Interbank Financial Transactions, which handles approximately one million messages each day. An Audit Commission report on computer crime concluded: 'Invariably the opportunity was provided because of a lack of basic controls rather than a particularly sophisticated manipulation of procedures. Generally speaking, the opportunity was blatant and weaknesses were known but for a variety of undisclosed reasons, management did not impose adequate controls.'

It may not just be information that the hacker is attempting to extract from your organization. It is possible that there is a desire to cause damage to the structure by altering files or installing computer viruses and other destructive elements. The criminal sanctions imposed under the Criminal Damage Act (1971) and the Computer Misuse Act (1990), which allows for three basic offences of unauthorized access to a computer, unauthorized access with intent to commit further crimes, and unauthorized modification of computer material, do not appear to be an adequate deterrent. The same is true in the USA, where the Computer Virus Eradication Act (1989) provides a penalty of up to fifteen years in gaol when losses are substantial.

Examples of devastating computer sabotage are legion, but some of the more colourful examples are listed below:

(a) The Logic Bomb. This is a delayed-reaction programme that is activated by an external event such as a date, name or an automatic count-down facility. The results can be total or partial destruction of files. An example of this device is the Michelangelo Virus (see above).

(b) The Trojan Horse. Named after its mythological equivalent, the system consists of a hidden piece of unorthodox but active code in a standard legitimate routine. As soon as the fraud has been initiated, the Trojan Horse will wipe itself out and vanish from the system.

(c) The Salami. The Salami 'slices' small sums of money from a large number of different bank accounts and automatically transfers the proceeds into an account controlled by the fraudster. It is similar to the rounding method mentioned earlier.

(d) Viruses. A computer virus is a special type of logic bomb that can copy itself to and from disks, into systems and across entire computer networks. It will often lie within a system until a set time or date, as in the case of the much-publicized Michelangelo Virus which was programmed to activate itself with devastating consequences on the anniversary of the painter's birthday. It is not just ruthless competitors who may employ such methods, but also individuals who may have moral reasons for attacking the company; for example, belligerent environmentalists concerned with dangerous emissions, or animal rights activists.

Corporate intelligence-gathering may also play tricks with computer hardware. For example, the combination of an inexpensive MW/AM-band radio, microphone and tape recorder, when placed near a computer, a telephone line or a modem, can pick up and record the sound of digital communications. Alternatively, one can use an inductive loop with a small low-gain amplifier near a telephone to record conversations. By identifying the pairs of tones being used, you can separate the caller and the host, record the transmissions and, by feeding the recorded tones into an oscilloscope, 'freeze' bits, words and characters. The start and stop bits can be stripped off and, with the help of a table to convert the system's binary transmissions into intelligible ASCII characters, you can examine what is happening.

TEMPEST/VDU RADIATION

Tempest denotes a series of US standards with set limits for the emission of electromagnetic radiation from computer systems. It is also known as 'Van Eck freaking' after William Van Eck, the Dutch scientist who first noticed the phenomenon.

It is possible to pick up images on a VDU screen from up to three hundred metres away from the target by tuning a suitable receiver to a VDU. All VDUs behave like a very crude television transmitter, with the signal being spread over a wide frequency band and not limited to one channel. The video elements displayed radiate harmonics on frequencies of 100–600 MHz. Use a domestic TV set and tune away from the signal and you will see electronic 'snow'. You should attach a mobile antenna and aim the aerial at the target VDU. You should see the 'snow' quality becoming brighter. The AM/MW receiver should now be set to between 1570 and 1600 KHz which will produce a buzzing sound that increases as you get closer to the VDU. This buzzing sound is the harmonic of the VDU's line synchronization.[3]

When eavesdropping in this way, the TV and MW radio are linked together with the MW radio pulses synchronizing the video elements being picked up by the TV screen. These can be recorded using a standard video recorder. The actual image produced will be the reverse of the norm, rather like looking in a mirror. As a result, black letters will appear on a lighter background. A similar technique is used by the TV detector vans that regularly patrol our streets.

Whilst Tempest works, its practical application is limited in the real world as it is expensive, the image can swim, and to get better reception means having to get too close to the target. The threat is therefore more perceived than real. A comparatively recent development in electronic transmissions is fibre-optic cables which, although harder to tap than conventional cables, can still fall victim to data interception. Johan Bergstrom, MSc, RIT, of Ericsson Business Communications AB, has described this happening in three ways as follows: 'Active tapping by connecting a repeater through which information may be retrieved. Passive tapping using a coupler. This is achieved by using a so-called "splitter" to tap part of the light transmitted in the fibre. If the transmitted signal is strong enough, the tapped light pulses can then be detected. Passive tapping using a detector . . . To tap in this way it is necessary to gain access to the bare fibres in the cable. The individual fibres are then bent with a very small bending radius, allowing some of the light to leak from the fibre core. This can be picked up by a detector placed very close to the fibre.'[4]

With computer systems becoming standard within businesses and the home, the threat of database spying is inevitably going to increase. Robert P. Campbell of Advanced Information Management, formerly head of security in the US Army, estimates that only one in a hundred computer crimes are detected. Of those detected, less than fifteen per cent are reported to the authorities, and of these only one in thirty-three is successfully prosecuted – producing a 'success rate of one in twenty-two thousand'.[5] This is hardly an impressive statistic and epitomizes the complacent attitude to security that exists in many companies. The next chapter will concentrate on advisable methods of improving computer security and countering the threat of computer espionage.

CHAPTER TWELVE

Computer Security and Counter-Measures

The condition upon which God hath given liberty
to man is eternal vigilance; which condition if he
break, servitude is at once the consequence of his
crime and the punishment of his guilt

John Philpot Curran[1]

The need for security has been acknowledged for millennia, and the development of the lock formalized this recognition. However, since the growth of information technology and the move away from tangible documents or files locked away each night in a filing cabinet, it seems that standards have slipped. The growth of 'invisible' data has made people relax their guard. This could have disastrous consequences for a company's profits and reputation.

Aside from the necessity of a company protecting itself from the effects of fraud or sabotage, one of the key principles of the Data Protection Act (1984) is that 'appropriate measures shall be taken against unauthorized access to, or alteration, disclosure or destruction of, personal data and against accidental loss or destruction of personal data.'[2] Therefore, the consequences for your company in allowing unauthorized access to personal data could be a claim in compensation for damages or distress suffered by the individual concerned, unless the company can prove it had taken such care as was reasonably required to prevent the loss, destruction, disclosure or access in question. This is a subjective test and, at the very least, it would bring unwelcome publicity to your organization.

Countering the threat of breaches in computer security

entails tackling the problem by a range of means from mundane methods of physical security to advanced counter-electronic measures. The recent case of the RAF officer who had his laptop computer, complete with Gulf War secrets, stolen from the boot of his car in west London should be a warning signal for senior company executives and salespeople who often travel with these devices as a matter of course. Increased security awareness and common sense are obvious preventative measures.

Other means of physical computer security include a keyboard lock, multi-level password systems, using PCs with built-in keypads enabling the user to key in a personal, preferably multi-level, code before access to the system is granted, and physically removing data from the computer. This latter system is common with floppy disks and the multi-surface disk packs used on mainframe computers, but more recently some systems are being introduced that will allow the hard disk to be removed from the computer. An analogy can be made with the increased use of removable stereo systems in motor vehicles. While some of these systems entail the risk of damage by constant jarring in the removal process, the more advanced ones are similar to the floppy disk principle, and allow the media to be removed from the computer while leaving the electronics and head mechanism behind. The data can be stored in a durable cartridge that self-seals against dust contamination when being transferred.

Wherever possible, computers and their support equipment should be placed in non-radiating and locked rooms where the mains supply is filtered. To prevent the possibility of terminal radiation you should use screened rooms with filters in the walls, although non-radiating terminals are now available. All signals sent by modem or directly onto a public network should be encoded using an appropriate encryption system. Where you have a local data network, you should screen the transmission cables and introduce special cable ducts to maximize security. Any connection points should also be secured against possible interception. A security adviser will have to present a convincing case to the board, as the costs are likely to be prohibitive. It is vital to make all parties aware of the immediate security costs when these are balanced against the potential costs of successful espionage activity.

Many of these problems can be solved by using fibre-optic cables, because this type of cable will not emit electromagnetic radiation. To tap a fibre-optic cable you would need to have physical access to every fibre in the cable, a technical nightmare that would involve considerable risks of detection. Although costly and requiring specialist help, the use of certain transmission equipment can make it impossible to mount a successful eavesdropping exercise.

Chapter 11 discussed three possible methods of tapping a fibre-optic link, but these methods are not infallible. When using a fibre-optic point-to-point link, the active transmission equipment has alarms designed to detect any problems on the cable, which means that any use of a coupler or a repeater by an eavesdropper will be detected. Passive tapping with a detector is very difficult and will entail the eavesdropper having physical access to the individual cable fibres. Often this will involve trespass, but there is also the risk of breaking the fibre when bending it, which could entail criminal damage and burglary as well as jeopardizing the mission.

To protect against this form of espionage you should use a cable shield or a security system integrated with an optical data link that continually monitors the state of the optical signal and activates an alarm as soon as it detects any tampering with the cable. An example of such an optical data link is the Erickson ZAT 4 DATA Security Link.

An additional level of security can be achieved by identifying 'footprints' on the installed cable using an Optical Time Domain Reflectometer (OTDR). The OTDR can produce a graphic display of the attenuation characteristics in the cable related to a distance. When the fibre link is disturbed, a new OTDR measurement can then be made. A comparison of the two measurements will reveal any change in the attenuation characteristics and thereby indicate the presence of a bug. The

OTDR system is very accurate and will also identify whether a coupler has been installed on the link. As a result of using high-tech fibre-optic links it is currently impossible to tap into a fibre-optic link with either a coupler or a detector without your activity being detected.

An effective method of protection against illegal access is by using a redial security system. These systems operate by connecting the dial-up modems and the computer and interrogating any incoming user to determine the user's name and access code. As soon as this task has been completed, the system will ask the user to 'hang up' and will then call him back from a number stored in its own database. If validation is successful, the machine can request an additional password before connecting the user to the computer system.

The better redial security systems use separate telephone lines for incoming and outgoing calls, and you should check that your access control system uses separate lines, as a single-line system can be conned into dialling back the incoming caller's telephone number. An added security factor is that the machine will assist in defining the modem ports but will not dial back on the modem that received the call. These systems can be instructed to grant access to a particular user only on certain days and at certain times, and will log all access attempts irrespective of their success. As access control is now performed from outside the computer, a hacker will not be able to 'cover his footprints', which will make detection easier. An example of this type of electronic security is the Ensign System 5000 produced by Ensign Communications Ltd.

Increasingly popular in commercial circles is the Electronic Data Interchange (EDI), but in the rush to embrace these advanced communication methods the opportunities for fraud are also increased. The growing use of EDI for financial payments is increasing the emphasis on security. EDIFACT (EDI for Administration, Commerce and Transport) has been developing a security framework to incorporate the use of digital signatures, which is likely to become the standard for the UK financial industry and internationally for EDI payment transactions between major corporations and the banks. Recent advances in cryptography will now allow access to the public key systems to be screened by production of a digital signature to authorize and confirm both the sender and his message.

There is no doubt that lax attitudes to security have cost industry millions of pounds in lost orders, and the effects of these losses on people's jobs can be tremendous. Computer fraud is increasing every day. In the words of Rupert Soames, managing director of GPT Data Systems, a division of GEC Plessey Telecommunications, in 1988: 'There has been a rapid increase in the number of hacking incidents during recent months. And, in the foreseeable future, hacking won't stop – mainly because networked systems remain so easy to penetrate.'[3]

CHAPTER THIRTEEN

The Seeing Eye – The Use of Cameras in Espionage

For I dipped into the future, far as human eye could
   see,
Saw a Vision of the world and all the wonder that
   would be . . .

Alfred Lord Tennyson[1]

No book on industrial espionage would be complete without mention of covert surveillance, and this work is no exception to the rule.

Photography has come a long way since its invention in the nineteenth century, but its application for covert uses was recognized early on and the past century has seen a frantic chase to outmanoeuvre the opposition in terms of perform-ance, technology and miniaturization. Some of the uses to which cameras have been put have been colourful. An example is the Brieftauben, Doppel-Sport or Pigeon Panoramic camera which dates from 1907 and was designed by Dr Julius Neubronner of Cronberg, Bavaria. According to Christie's photographic historian, Michael Pritchard, Neubronner intro-duced a carrier-pigeon postal service for the transmission of medical prescriptions between a Falkenstein hospital and his pharmacist's shop. The camera was developed to be carried by these pigeons to undertake aerial photography and was tested at the carrier-pigeon station at the Ministry of War in Spandau, but 'was found to be without practical value'.[2] Nevertheless, it remains a colourful example of creative thought. The more recent advent of fibre-optics, 'magic eye' cameras, and under-water and satellite remote sensing could only have been imag-ined by the likes of Jules Verne a hundred years ago, yet such systems now exist and are often used in the world of industrial espionage.

SPY CAMERAS

Undoubtedly the camera most identified with espionage is the Minox. In the words of Morris Moses: 'Secrets, espionage, counter-espionage: the tiny Minox conjures up visions of trench coats, wide-brim hats, secret missions, danger, excite-ment and trepidation . . . the tortuous history of the Minox rivals any adventure movie in its geographic settings and the surrounding world events.'[3] The Minox is the world's smallest high-precision camera and is unrivalled in its performance and tenacity. The original Minox was first produced in Riga, Latvia by Walter Zapp, a largely self-educated man who reduced a standard 35mm film size by seventy-five per cent to reach a film size of 8.75mm, with the final film proportions measuring just 6.5 by 9mm. The first ever Minox was the 'Ur Minox', but the first of the cameras to be mass-produced was the 'Riga Minox' by VEF (Valsts Electrotechniska Fabrika), an indepen-dent Latvian state enterprise, in 1939 – an unfortunate time to launch a new product with World War II beginning in September of that year. Walter Zapp and his Minox camera survived occupation by both Nazi and Soviet forces and the cameras are still produced in Germany today.

The innovative aspects of the Minox include its size and weight. During the 1950s an American model called Mary Ann Lejoy was photographed with a Minox camera used as both an earring and a necklace. Another innovative feature is the use of a special measuring chain containing beads located at regular intervals, to help with measuring distance for close-ups. Non-metric chains had intervals of 8, 10, 12 and 18 inches, while the metric chains used intervals of 20, 24, 30 and 40cm. A comparison may be drawn with the way in which an artist extends his arm to its full length and moves it up and down the length of the pencil to measure distance in relation to perspective.

History is littered with examples of the Minox camera in use. Early in May 1940, John Moore-Brabazon secretly photographed the House of Commons in session during the debate on the Norwegian campaign. In 1949, James 'Mad Dog' Morelli, a notorious Chicago gangster, was executed 'in camera'. A particularly tenacious reporter called Joe Mignon smuggled a Minox in his shoe into the execution chamber. The resulting picture produced a media 'scoop' for the *Chicago Herald*. The movies are no exception, with James Stewart using a Minox in *Call Northside 777* in 1948 and Walter Matthau using one in the 1980 film *Hopscotch*. It goes without saying that James Bond has used the camera in covert photography.

Occasionally, spy cameras have been used in bizarre ways. For example, Clayton Hutton, a former member of the MI9 escape group during World War II, adapted the Minox into a cigarette lighter by using a Bowers-type lighter made by Blunts of London. Not wishing to be outdone, the Japanese company Suzuki Optical Works began making petrol cigarette lighters and cameras, such as the 'Echo 8'. Cigarette-lighter cameras are still popular. In reality, a camera can be built into any normal receptacle, obvious ones including briefcases, handbags, and radio/cassette recorders. Various examples of such camera receptacles can be found in the illustrated section.

Cigarette packets make ideal receptacles for miniature cameras, and one of the most collectable is the 16mm metal-body Lucky Strike cigarette-packet camera. The Lucky Strike Spy Camera was developed for the US Signal Corps between 1949 and 1959 by Mast Development Corp. Inc. and comprised a five-element f/2.7 17.5mm Sonnar-type lens, a 16mm film capable of eighteen exposures, and had a focal-plane shutter mounted in front of the lens and shutter speeds of B, 1/15, 1/250 and 1/500. Most of the more popular brands of cigarette packet have been used as camera receptacles. A good example of their use occurred in the late 1970s when a photographer managed to take a blurred snapshot of the decapitation of an errant Saudi Arabian princess which was reproduced on the front page of a prominent UK newspaper. The photograph caused a sensation and led to the TV documentary 'Death of a Princess'.

Cameras have also been built into wristwatches, pocket watches, ballpoint pens, buttons, tie-pins, radios and rings. Another of the more prolific manufacturers of spy cameras was Petie, who designed several cameras that were built into ladies' vanity cases, complete with black crackle-and-chrome metal body with a 25mm f/11 lens, film holder, lipstick holder, and powder compact. For the gentleman, one can buy a Ben Akiba walking-stick camera with polished chrome-plated body, decorative engraving, film-winding key, shutter, lens, and five internally contained film spools – an example is included among the illustrations.

While originally not designed as a spy camera, Minox was soon to exploit the market identified with its products and in 1979 ran an advertising campaign showing a lady's eyes partly obscured by the rim of a fedora hat with the following slogan underneath: 'The Minox spy camera . . . It's not just for beautiful spies any more'. Of all spy cameras, the Minox is regarded as the most enduring. In the words of the camera's biographer, Morris Moses: 'Users [have] included people from all walks of life, and the amount of documented lore surrounding the Minox is endless. The camera has been used to steal military secrets, as well as commercial secrets worth millions of dollars. The Minox has saved the lives of people trapped underground, and . . . has also been responsible for helping to bring a priceless art treasure to the Metropolitan Museum of Art in New York City.'[4]

CONVENTIONAL PHOTOGRAPHY

It is far more common for industrial spies or plain 'snoopers' to use standard 35mm-mode single-lens reflex cameras, albeit with high performance and a spectacular array of lenses. Such cameras can be adapted into normal receptacles such as shoulder-bags, briefcases or attaché cases, with an extension cord linking the shutter mechanism to a prestle (compression) switch built into the handle – just point and press; the obligatory automatic winder will do the rest. Naturally, it is important for you to practise your photographic angles and remember to count the number of pictures you have taken, as it is easy to lose count and a cursory check of the film-number counter could easily give you away.

There are also more specialized 35mm cameras that possess additional advantages, such as silenced operations, high film capacity, small dimensions, fast sequence operation through automatic film transport, electric camera release, and radio release at remote distances. An excellent manufacturer of such products, often with discreet receptacles provided, is the Dusseldorf-based firm of Robot Foto und Electronics Gmbh, 'the trademark of photographic automation and instrumentalization'. One of their most useful products is a mobile reprographic unit that works independently of a mains supply or local lighting conditions. The device is disguised in a normal attaché case and requires no particular photographic skills to be operated.

One of the most useful sources of information on covert photography and video is the annual Covert and Operational Procurement Exhibition (Copex), held in both the UK and the USA. The three-day event describes itself as 'the definitive showcase of internal security, counter-insurgency and special operations equipment and services for end users worldwide'. While the products advertised include weapons, riot-control equipment, radios, anti-terrorist and intelligence equipment, and a host of other security products, many companies that specialize in thermal imaging devices and electro-optics take part. Night-vision scopes and infra-red cameras, all utilizing the latest in technology, are demonstrated, along with micro-lenses used for wall penetration. Some firms will prefer to know who they are dealing with before they reveal too much, especially as some of these products may be purchased by certain government departments.

Which films to use in your photography will depend on prevailing weather conditions. The Minox has its own size of film, but within the general 35mm range it is important to remember that one should use a higher ASA when lighting conditions are poor. The following ASA ranges are readily available commercially: 100, 200, 400, 1000 and 2000. Others can of course be obtained from specialist sources. It is impor-tant to remember that poor lighting conditions will require not just a slower film (higher ASA) but also a much longer exposure. Always make sure that the camera is fixed for the duration of the exposure to avoid any blurring of the finished product.

The advent of the video has altered much in photographic surveillance, especially as such devices can be left for long periods of time in concealed locations and do not have to have their films changed after 'n' exposures – especially so with the introduction of the 'magic eye' movement detector. If operating internationally it is important to ensure that your video system is compatible with local systems, such as the American PAL video system. Poor light can be compensated for by using infra-red cameras or night scopes that 'lock on' to light from all available sources. A popular device is 'Star-light', so called because of its ability to utilize light emanating from stars.

SATELLITE PHOTOGRAPHY

Let observation with extensive view
Survey mankind, from China to Peru
Samuel Johnson[5]

Mankind is always seeking new methods of gaining aerial information. One way has been to use altitude, by means of balloons or aeroplanes, or even by employing homing pigeons to fly above an area with a camera strapped to their underbelly, as the earlier example illustrated.[6] During World War II, photo reconnaissance aircraft carrying infra-red sensitive film were able to detect camouflaged enemy vehicles which gave off considerably more heat than real foliage. In 1957 the Soviets launched the world's first satellite, and the past thirty years have witnessed a massive rethink in how aerial data is collected.

Satellite remote sensing gathers information invisible to the human eye by increasing both spatial and spectral reach through the collection of information from the infra-red areas of the electromagnetic spectrum. Sensors are designed to be responsive to different areas of the spectrum. All satellite remote sensing is digital in origin. Scanners numerically record radiation from the Earth's surface and transmit this to a receiving station as numbers. Computers then generate the image we see via image-enhancement technology.[7]

It is common knowledge that the spy satellite took over the traditional role of the 'U-2' spy planes and their Soviet equivalents. William S. Burroughs' book *Deep Black* specifically refers to the use of 'crate-ology' (a term that was also used in the 1992 BBC documentary on the CIA) during the 1962 Cuban Missile Crisis. Burroughs defines 'crate-ology' as using spy satellites to photograph crates on board Cuban-bound Soviet ships.[8] It was then the CIA's job to identify the contents of these crates. The same exercise can be applied in standard corporate intelligence-gathering, especially as regards assessing a company's physical stocks. American photographic surveillance via spy satellite is interpreted and evaluated by the National Reconnaissance Office and the National Photographic Interpretation Centre, which are closely allied to Defense. However, there are other agencies, such as the Environmental Protection Agency (EPA) and the Environmental Photographic Interpretation Centre (EPIC), which use spy planes to map areas of toxic risk. Their data represents an ideal form of cartographic intelligence for the corporate spy and is readily available thanks to the Freedom of Information Act.

Satellite photography is now commercially available for a fee both in the USA, from its 'Landset' satellite, and in Europe from the French 'Spot' satellites which use a tracking station in Toulouse. 'Spot 1' was launched in 1986 and 'Spot 2' in 1990. These satellites scan the whole earth every twenty-six days and can provide ten-metre images in black and white and twenty-metre colour photographs. All the satellite images are transmitted to and processed by the tracking station near Toulouse where they are sold commercially for map-making, agriculture and mineral exploration work, as well as for other undisclosed reasons. Great embarrassment was caused to the 'Spot' programme when it was revealed that the organization had sold maps of Kuwait and Saudi Arabia to Saddam Hussein prior to the Iraqi invasion of Kuwait in August 1990. The final set of photographs was delivered to Iraq on 2 May 1990. It is planned to launch two further Spot satellites as the millennium approaches.

Even the EC has begun to use satellite espionage to counter the problem of fraudulent claims under the Common Agricultural Policy. The MARS (Monitoring Agriculture with Remote Sensing) project was established to demonstrate how remote sensing could be used to help combat this form of fraud. Satellites spy on farmers to ensure that they are not claiming EC subsidies for crops that they are not actually growing.[9] Obviously, such means of corporate intelligence-gathering are draconian and expensive, and more conventional methods will generally suffice. However, more participants are coming into the market, and it is likely that the need for hard currency will force the Russians to transform their space programme into a more commercial enterprise. Already, a British company called Sigma Products has been awarded a contract with Soyuzkarta, the Soviet agency responsible for mapping and remote sensing, to market their satellite-produced photographs. It is believed that the Mir space station can produce satellite photographs down to an image refinement of five metres. Of course, quality can be refined further by using computers to enhance images.

POLAROID CAMERAS

Assuming that you have been granted entry to premises and have the time to examine the area thoroughly, it is wise to carry a Polaroid camera with plenty of film and spare batteries to enable you to take 'before and after' photographs when moving furniture or the contents of drawers. Naturally, this sort of activity carries with it numerous risks of detection, and the consequences of discovery should be borne in mind. The author advises those intending to implement this practice to do so only when granted special permission by company directors to investigate an errant employee, and never to remove property. The advantage of a Polaroid camera is that all angles of furniture and positions of documents can be 'frozen' and everything replaced exactly as it was before the inspection began. It is wise to perform this exercise in a logical manner, starting from left to right and controlling personnel closely. Always ensure that curtains or blinds are drawn as a Polaroid camera will give off a powerful flash that could attract unwanted attention.

CHAPTER FOURTEEN

Government-Sponsored Corporate Espionage

Who steals my purse steals trash . . .
But he that filches from me my good name
Robs me of that which not enriches him,
And makes me poor indeed

William Shakespeare[1]

The government of the former Soviet Union has, during the twentieth century, been the most notorious of governments for sponsoring industrial espionage. Before the demise of the USSR, West German intelligence managed to obtain a copy of the 'Red Book', which was a KGB 'shopping list', constantly updated, from which agents were expected to procure four items each year. The official title of this book was *Coordinated Requests for Technical Information*, and the compilers of the lists were the VPK, or Military-Industrial Commission of the USSR.[2] The book consisted of twenty-seven chapters and covered computers, robotics, artificial intelligence, lasers, genetic engineering, radar and infra-red sensors, fibre-optics, space technology, aerodynamics, telecommunication advances and propulsion techniques, as well as a host of other fields. Little is known of the VPK, other than that certain of their members held ministerial and Politburo rank. Their influence was vast and their demands were sifted through official bodies, principally the KGB, GRU, Ministry of Foreign Trade, USSR Academy of Sciences, and the State Committee for Science and Technology.

A report prepared by the CIA on VPK activities stated that: 'In certain of the [technical] areas, notably the development of microelectronics, the Soviets would have been incapable of achieving their present technical level without the acquisition of Western technology. This advance comes as a result of over ten years of successful acquisition – through illegal, including clandestine, means, of hundreds of pieces of Western microelectronic equipment with hundreds of millions of dollars to equip their military-related manufacturing facilities. These acquisitions have permitted the Soviets to systematically build a microelectronics industry which will be the critical basis for enhancing the sophistication of future military systems for decades. The acquired equipment and know-how, if combined, could meet 100% of the Soviets' high-quality microelectronic needs for military purposes or 50% of all their microelectronic needs.'[3] Indeed, 2790 Green Street, Pacific Heights, San Francisco was the most important Soviet consulate in the world owing to its proximity to Silicon Valley. An incongruous hi-tech hut situated on the roof could intercept telephone conversations and beam them up to an orbiting spy satellite via the 'burst' transmission system. It is impossible to calculate how much this has cost the US computer industry.

Totalitarian regimes are invariably associated with industrial espionage as it is the cheapest form of research and development, and the methods are already well practised in these nations. However, Western-style democracies are also much to blame, and we ignore the threat posed by our 'friends' and 'allies' at our peril.

France and Japan are typical examples of nations who test the bonds of 'friendship' by their corporate intelligence spying. In France, the General Department for External Security is involved in industrial espionage, and allegations abound of French 'moles' in the overseas offices of various American blue-chip companies. Indeed, more recently, allegations have been made of French industrial spies posing as flight attendants and bugging aeroplanes to see what they could glean from international business travellers. A former member of the French intelligence agency has recently confirmed these allegations. The Department is likely to increase its corporate spying activities in the future to protect French industry from overseas predators and to analyse commercial opportunities in Eastern Europe.[4]

Japan's enormous corporate intelligence networks date back to the end of World War II, when many Japanese military intelligence specialists found themselves redundant and assisted in the reconstruction of the Japanese economy. Later, many went to work for Japan's vast trading companies, and nowadays it is these same companies that form the basis of Japan's massive commercial intelligence system.[5] Much of the Japanese government's corporate intelligence work is sponsored by the Japanese External Trade Organization (JETRO) and the Ministry of International Trade and Industry (MITI). JETRO's Ryuchi Hattori[6] has said that a key to Japan's success is the way in which competitor intelligence is delivered to decision-makers, with most Japanese employees stationed overseas responsible for gathering information and reporting it on a scheduled basis. Jan Herring of the Futures Group has said of US firms that only three per cent have divisions dedicated to competitor intelligence systems, which contrasts with one hundred per cent of Japanese companies.[7]

During the 1950s, 1960s and 1970s, Japanese intelligence-gatherers would concentrate on the United States for their technical information, but as they have surged so far ahead in these technical fields their corporate intelligence work during the 1980s and 1990s has concentrated more on gaining information on US lifestyles for their marketing strategies.[8] A recent well-publicized example of lifestyle analysis occurred in 1989, when a Nissan employee called Takashi Morimoto rented a room in Costa Mesa in California from a US family and used the experience to perform market research. The Japanese will collect data on almost any subject and have been called 'information barracudas' by Thomas Zengage, a partner at International Business Information, which is a research and consulting firm based in Tokyo. The latest focus for their attacks are research and consulting laboratories at American and European universities. Already, at Stanford University, various Japanese companies have endowed six permanent chairs and one visiting professorship in business studies and engineering. This trend is likely to continue for the foreseeable future.

The USA, UK and other leading Western democracies have been slow to acknowledge the threats posed by corporate intelligence spies, but that is all rapidly changing. In the words of David L. Boren (Democrat, Oklahoma), Chairman of the Senate Intelligence Committee: 'Going into the next century our position of world leadership will depend more on our economic strength than even our military strength.'[9]

The Central Intelligence Agency (CIA) is currently forbidden by law to provide information directly to US corporations, although many people feel that the law should be amended given the shift away from a global communist threat and the concentration on economic espionage. Ray Cline, a former deputy director of the CIA and now Chairman of the US Global Strategy Council, suggests that the American international community should focus more on international economics, which would help the competitiveness of American business.[10] Others are more forthright — Admiral Stansfield Turner, who was in charge of the CIA under the Carter Administration, has said: 'We steal secrets for our military preparedness. I don't see why we shouldn't to stay economically competitive.' His views are echoed by the former trade negotiator, Michael B. Smith, who has said: 'Other countries have active intelligence programmes directed against our companies to give their companies a leg up. We ought to emulate them.'[11]

Under the new director of the CIA, Robert M. Gates, many intelligence and trade experts see an opportunity for a radical change in CIA objectives. Under Gates, it is likely that the CIA will recruit more economists, seek to eradicate foreign practices that harm US corporations, and work to counter the theft of US technology and trade secrets by overseas corporations and foreign governments.[12,13] This change in emphasis is taking place in other countries as well. Roger Faligot, a French authority on intelligence agencies, has commented:

'Intelligence will be increasingly used to gain advantages in breaking into markets abroad, particularly in Eastern Europe.'

That the vast American industrial machine is at last beginning to awaken to the threat posed by corporate intelligence-gathering is seen in the way in which US corporations are now going on the offensive and becoming adept at legal methods of gathering information on their competitors. Nutrasweet now has a 'Strategic and Business Information Group' which recently began building personal profiles of their competitors' key decision-makers to try to predict their strategic moves. Prime Computer has a manager of 'Competitor Intelligence and Sales Analysis' for their computerization unit who is responsible for the collection of information on their competitors' sales and product development. The company Helene Curtis has created a new 'strategy and productivity development' department which employs former military personnel who are instructed to build up intelligence information to cut costs and improve quality. Kodak[14] and AT & T are now actively pursuing pro-active research programmes, and a company called Corning encourages all its employees to send information on rival companies to a central database where the data is analysed and distributed to the entire workforce.[15]

An example of corporate intelligence-gathering is the campaign allegedly conducted by the Marriott hotel group. According to Brian Dumaine, in 1986 employees of Marriott hotels checked into a rival hotel in Atlanta, Georgia and began a thorough secret intelligence-gathering mission to glean as much information as possible about one of Marriott's potential rivals. Recordings were made of a couple making love in the next room to assess the sound-proofing of each room. Copious notes were made on soap and shampoo brands, notepaper and towels. Once all this data was processed, Marriott budgeted $500 million for their new-model hotel chain to rival their competitor in every respect. The result was Fairfield Inns, with an occupancy rate ten per cent higher than the rest of the market.[16]

It is now time for the UK to discard its obsession with playing by a defined but unwritten rule-book of gentlemanly behaviour and take measures to stem the flow of information from company premises while ensuring that business people can procure as much information as possible from their competitors.

CHAPTER FIFTEEN

Conclusion – The Future

The seed ye sow, another reaps;
The wealth ye find, another keeps;
The robes ye weave, another wears;
The arms ye forge, another bears.
Percy Bysshe Shelley[1]

Corporate intelligence-gathering is a growth industry. The threat comes not just from government-sponsored sources but also from private companies themselves. Every week millions of pounds are lost through the theft of secrets, counterfeit products swamping the market, reverse engineering, disinformation campaigns, and through a host of other methods detailed in this book.

The former Soviet Union was probably the world's greatest exponent of industrial espionage. This opinion is supported by the words of General Leonid Shobasishin, the former Deputy Chief of the KGB's First Chief Directorate: 'The Soviets' main task is to keep track of events and developments by the collection of military, strategic, political, economic and counter-espionage information. Overt collection is not enough – a State's secrets are secret, but if they affect the Soviet Union especially, will be used when there is no other way.'[2]

The Soviet Union's demise, though welcome, must not be an excuse for lowering our guard against the threat of foreign intelligence agencies. If anything, the now semi-redundant KGB will reduce their domestic espionage activity to the sound of universal applause from the West and will metamorphose into an economic espionage network to concentrate on commercial intelligence-gathering.

A parallel can be drawn with what occurred in Japan after their ignominious defeat at the end of World War II. The countries of the Commonwealth of Independent States (CIS) are countries that dramatically lag behind the West in technology, but they will catch up rapidly. The threat of corporate espionage is now far greater than it has ever been because state-sponsored corporate intelligence-gathering will gradually become dwarfed by pure corporate intelligence-gathering. In the words of Nicholas van der Bijl: 'The current upsurge in Soviet espionage is, I believe, unlikely to diminish and it will continue to cost the West dear to protect its secrets. Business must continue to regard the Commonwealth of Independent States as an equal threat to the Soviet Union, until the espionage climate changes.'[3] With the likelihood of reduced labour costs in the new democracies of Eastern Europe, and their eventual inevitable capacity to undercut our own prices, we ignore these risks at our peril.

While there is now pressure for the CIA to come to the aid of American business, there can be no guarantee that the same will happen with MI5 and MI6 in the United Kingdom. Indeed, MI5 has only recently taken on the mantle of countering the threat from the IRA. Even countries that have traditionally enjoyed the support of their intelligence agencies in economic matters cannot rely on that support continuing or ever being fully comprehensive.

True competitor intelligence can only be undertaken realistically at corporate level. There are signs that some countries are beginning to wake up to this. These initiatives must not only be maintained but should be actively encouraged. Specialist departments for corporate intelligence-gathering should be established, and the roles of libraries within companies be given enhanced and pro-active status. Overall company security must be improved and regular security audits carried out. If necessary, technology must be installed to counter likely threats. However, the fundamental factor always to be borne in mind is the fallibility of employees. All employees must be given a sense of pride in the company; they must feel wanted and useful. Above all, staff must be educated in the risks inherent in breaches of security and learn to recognize that the consequences of such a breach would be immediate dismissal.

Legislation *per se* will not prevent corporate spying, nor should it be introduced except to counter the threats posed by electronic espionage. The selective exchange of information is a healthy practice in a democracy and a welcome gesture of cohesion for the human race, but it must be undertaken in a controlled atmosphere with the role of the security adviser given enhanced status. Prevention is better than cure, and effective prevention can only come about through adequate investment in a corporate intelligence department with both a pro-active research and a counter-espionage function.

World War III is the global war of industrial espionage; it is an undeclared war that began many years ago but, unlike other wars, it will never end. There is no absolute solution to the problem, but the effects of industrial espionage can be prevented if sensible precautions are taken. It is hoped that this book will go some way towards helping to solve the problem.

APPENDICES

Appendix 1 Glossary of terms and City words
Appendix 2 List of useful sources mentioned in text
Appendix 3 List of prominent electronic database producers
            and their capabilities
Appendix 4 List of additional useful information sources:
            (a) Newsletters
            (b) Stockbrokers providing reports and analyses
            (c) Economic trends and forecasts
            (d) Directories
            (e) CD-ROM information sources
Appendix 5 List of statutes found in the text

APPENDIX 1

Glossary of terms and City words

Active	Used in relation to an agent who is currently involved in a venture.
AFBD	Association of Futures Brokers and Dealers, which merged with the Security Association (TSA) in April 1991 to form the Securities and Futures Authority (SFA).
Agent	A human information source who can provide information either unwittingly or with full knowledge of what he is doing. Can be active or passive.
Amplifier	An electrical circuit which makes a small signal larger by increasing the power supply.
Analyst	An intelligence operative who collects and collates information from varying sources.
Answer mode	Where a modem has been set up to receive calls.
Asset tracing	Undertaken mainly by security consultants or private investigators to locate assets after a fraud has been established or as a preemptive method of deciding whether a person is worth suing.
Asynchronous	A system of 'start' and 'stop' bits used in electronic communications to synchronize the originator and receiver of data.
Audio compressor	Assists in levelling out different sound volumes and is attached between the microphone and the transmitter or recorder.
Audio spectrum	The full range of space available for radio transmissions. Measured in megahertz and kilohertz.
Audit	A detailed financial analysis provided by independent experts.
Autodialler	An automated method of fast communications dialling. Used as an accessory to a modem link.

Bibliography	A market term referring to a general synopsis of an individual or an institution often leading to more in-depth information later.
Big Bang	The expression given to the deregulation of the UK financial markets which occurred in October 1986.
Box 500	MI5.
Bug	A generic term for eavesdropping devices.
Burst	A term given to an accelerated coded transmission system used by the SAS. Also known as 'Spurt'.
Captive insurance company	A subsidiary of another company which is wholly owned by a non-insurance company and which conducts business exclusively to underwrite the insurable risks of its parent or its associated companies.
Case officer	A controller of an intelligence brief responsible for all field agents.
CD-ROM	Compact Disk – Read Only Memory. A system of electronic retrieval from a database held in CD format.
Cheesebox	An automatic telephone director which is attached to the telephone and automatically redirects any incoming calls to a pre-set number without the caller being aware of the fact.
Chinese Walls	A post-Big Bang system of imaginary barriers said now to exist within the City of London securities dealing-rooms to prevent buyers and sellers of information sharing that information and creating a conflict of interest.
CIA	Central Intelligence Agency – the American Secret Service.
Cleanse	To sanitize a place or area so that no incriminating evidence remains.
Clocked	To be seen by the target, which means that the operative concerned must be replaced or surveillance abandoned.
Close company	A registered company having five or fewer members.
The Company	A colloquial term for the CIA.
Competitor intelligence	See Corporate intelligence.

Conglomerate	A corporate entity that is made up of many varied and unrelated areas of business.
Control	A central communications point used by all operatives assigned to a set project.
Corporate intelligence	The method of obtaining information on one's competitors by fair and foul means. Also known as pro-active market research and competitor intelligence.
Corporate raiders	The term given to those who launch hostile takeover bids in mergers and acquisitions.
Counter-intelligence/ espionage	A system designed to counter the threat posed by hostile forces.
Cover	A pretext to protect one's true identity.
Covert	The conduct of investigations by discreet and normally undetectable methods.
Crate-ology	A CIA term for assessing the contents of crates or boxes by their size, shape, position and frequency. The system was used very successfully during the Cuban Missile Crisis.
Cryptology	The preparation and transmission of coded messages.
Dawn raid	When a buyer of shares in a target company buys up a large shareholding as soon as trading starts in the morning by offering a premium price as an inducement.
DB/DP	Direction Box/Direction Point. A centralized telephone area containing several connections for the surrounding telephone lines.
Dead letter box	An address considered safe from unwarranted enquiries. Often used in false-flag or sting operations.
Dead cat bounce	The short-term illusion of a recovery in a falling stock market.
Desk-man	A person who works as an analyst or an investigator within the confines of an office.
Disinformation	A popular method of discrediting one's opposition or competitors by spreading false or malicious rumours as to product safety and reliability.
Double agent	An agent whose loyalty is only to himself and who acts for and against both sides in an intelligence operation.
Dow Jones	The index of US security prices.
Drive past	Used as a surveillance method in performing a reconnaisance.

Drop point	An area or a place used to pass information or material discreetly.
DTP	Desk Top Publishing.
Due diligence	An enquiry into an individual or institution to check verifiable facts.
Duplex	A system of bi-directional transmission, such as a telephone.
E-Mail	Computer-based electronic mail.
Echo	A repetition of sound produced by sound waves reflected from an object denser than the aerial medium.
ECU	European Currency Unit.
EDI	Electronic Data Interchange.
EMS	European Monetary System.
ERM	Exchange Rate Mechanism.
False-flag	A method of obtaining information by means of a pretext, often with supporting documentation. Also known as a 'sting' operation.
The Farm	CIA training area at Williamsburg, Virginia.
Feedback detector	A device used for the detection of radio transmitter bugs which relies on the regeneration of a signal.
Fibre-optics	Glass fibres which are used to carry light energy.
Field	The term used to denote work outside the office.
Field Strength Meter	An electronic radio field detection device which detects the presence of broadband RF energy.
FIMBRA	Financial Intermediaries, Managers and Brokers Regulatory Association – a self-regulatory organization covering the life assurance and unit trust industry. It was set up by the Financial Services Act (1986). Soon to form part of the new Personal Investment Authority (PIA).
FOCC	Forward Control Channel.
Footsie	Financial Times-Stock Exchange 100 Share Index.
Frame-room	The area of a building which houses the central telephone line coordination point for the premises. It is normally located in the basement area.
Free spirit	A freelancer who works on an ad hoc basis.

Frequency equalizer	This complements an audio compressor and helps to focus key conversations by eliminating background noises.
FSA	Financial Services Act (1986), which formalized the concept of a self-regulatory market overseen by the Securities and Investment Board.
FVC	Forward Voice Channel.
G7	Group of the seven richest nations in the world.
Gateway	An entry point into a computer network.
Ghost	A colloquial term used for an intelligence officer. Often used for embassy staff with a dual function.
Greenmail	When a predator purchases shares in a target company which then buys them back at a higher price to avoid the predator.
Grey market	The unofficial price quoted for shares before they are officially advertised for sale in the Stock Exchange.
GRU	*Glavnoye Razedyvatelnoye Upravleniye*. The Chief Intelligence Directorate of Soviet General Staff.
Hacking	Unauthorized access to computer systems.
Handshake	Computer-speak for the system of electronic communications between computers.
Homer/Homing device	A beacon which transmits a signal that can be picked up by a receiver. Often used to identify the location of vehicles.
Honeypot	The planting of fake information to be used to ensnare an agent. Often used as part of a false-flag or sting operation.
Hookswitch defeat	A system to prevent the handset of a telephone being replaced correctly across the hookswitch, thereby holding the line open as a listening device.
Host	A computer network housing several databases which acts as an intermediary between the producer and the client.
IMRO	Investment Management Regulatory Organization – a self-regulatory organization monitoring investment trusts and pension funds introduced as a result of the Financial Services Act (1986).

Inductive tap	A cheap form of bug consisting of a small cylinder with two wires at one end and a rubber sticker on the other end. Rather obvious and therefore of limited use. Operates on the principle of electromagnetic induction.
Infinite device	A small transmitter which uses a phone line and telephone to tap a room. The infinite device is activated by means of a tone signal being sent down the line to a receiving unit.
Insider dealing	The illegal practice of using unlisted price-sensitive information to one's own advantage. Now given express statutory sanction by the Insider Dealing Act (1986).
Into play	When a predator buys a stake in a company, the company is said to come into play.
Invisible data	Information held electronically which because of its 'invisibility' has made many employees less security-conscious.
IOSCO	International Organization of Securities Commissions.
Jammer	A device used to block or interfere with the transmission or reception of radio traffic.
JETRO	Japanese External Trade Association.
Junk bonds	High-risk, high-yield unsecured bonds used in buy-outs in the USA.
Keypad	A numeric or alphabetic method of communicating with a computer system.
KGB	*Komitet Gosudarstvennoy Bezopasnoti*. The clandestine Soviet Security Service.
LAN	Local Area Network.
Laser bug	A device that picks up sound vibrations as they hit a surface such as glass.
Laundering	The ability to disguise illegally obtained money from the attentions of regulatory authorities.
LAUTRO	Life Assurance and Unit Trust Regulatory Organisation – a self-regulatory organization responsible for monitoring pooled investments. Soon to form part of the new Personal Investment Authority (PIA).

LBO	Leveraged buy-out – borrowing heavily so as to be able to buy assets with the assets being used as security for the loan.
Legend	A detailed cover-story.
LIBOR	London Inter-Bank Offered Rate – the interest rate applied by London banks when they lend to each other.
Lifestyle check	Similar to a due-diligence enquiry – a thorough check on an individual or an institution.
LIFFE	London International Financial Futures Exchange, which covers the future price of interest rates and currencies.
LME	London Metal Exchange.
Logic bomb	A hostile and alien computer programme which will normally destroy computer files by using a delayed-reaction system.
Machine-gun mike	A long-distance microphone consisting of a series of small cups mounted along a central tube.
Market-making	System introduced to replace the separated functions of stockbroking and stockjobbing after the Big Bang of October 1986.
MBI	Management buy-in. An outside management team buys a business with assistance from financial backers.
MBO	Management buy-out. A company's management buys the business with assistance from financial backers.
MI5	The UK's domestic secret intelligence service. Also known as Box 500.
MI6/SIS	The UK's overseas secret intelligence service.
Microfiche	A miniaturized storage system which uses sheets of plastic as the storage medium. A microfiche reader will be required; these are commercially available.
Microfilm	A filmed miniaturized storage system normally using reels of microfilm. Also used in microphotography.
MITI	Japanese Ministry of International Trade and Industry.
Mole	A person who is able to infiltrate an organization using a cover-story.
MOU	Memorandum of Understanding on Mutual Assistance and Exchange of

	Information. Occasionally signed by the Securities and Investment Board, the DTI and the equivalent regulatory bodies in overseas countries.
NBT	Not Before Time – products which are felt to have a promising future.
Nikkei	Tokyo Stock Exchange.
Non-linear junction detector	Counter-measure equipment which uses semiconductor junctions to produce resonant harmonics when near a UHF or microwave signal.
Offshore haven	An area of the world which is popular for tax-avoidance schemes as well as hiding assets which might otherwise come to the attention of regulatory authorities.
OFT	Office of Fair Trading, which determines competition policy.
On-line	The term given to electronic database systems when in operation.
Optical discs	These are high-density storage devices which hold machine-readable data. An example is CD-ROM.
Oscillator	Electrical circuit which produces an audio tone or a radio-frequency carrier.
OTDR	Optical Time Domain Reflectometer.
Overt	Open methods of intelligence-gathering, such as via reference libraries.
PABX	Private Automatic Branch Exchange.
Parabolic mike	A large metal or plastic dish which reflects sound towards the microphone in the centre.
Parallel radio tap	A transmitter device which is attached across the wires of a telephone line.
Passive	Used in the context of an agent whose services are not currently required but will be required in the future, or an agent who is oblivious as to his being used.
PBX	Private Branch Exchange.
Phoenixism	Businesses which go into voluntary liquidation to evade tax and national insurance obligations.
Pin-hole	A small hole through which a tiny fibre-optic camera can protrude. Also a type of camera.
Poison pill	A defensive method used by the victim of a takeover battle against the predator which

	causes the victim's assets automatically to reduce in value as soon as the predator gains control.
Polarisation	When two or more concepts or opinions are 'poles apart', i.e. totally diverse.
Polaroid	An instant camera of great use for conducting on-site searches to ensure that everything is left just as it should have been.
Prestel	The Post Office electronic information system.
Pretext	A background cover-story to assist in gaining access to a target's premises.
Protocol	An agreed set of rules.
PSTN	Public Switched Telephone Network.
Psychographics	The system of looking at consumer behaviour to assist in corporate intelligence-gathering for marketing strategy.
Pulse generator	An electronic device used to activate a receiver mecnanism. More modern telephones respond to a tone-generated system.
RCC	Reverse Control Channel.
RDF	Radio Direction-Finding.
The Regiment	Colloquial name for the SAS.
Relay	A system used to boost transmission distances, occasionally used in vehicles.
RF flooding	A method of room eavesdropping that sends a radio frequency (RF) carrier along a telephone line to activate the handset microphone in the telephone.
Rifle mike	A directional microphone used predominately outdoors. Good for long-distance reception. The system bears an uncanny resemblance to a rifle – hence the name.
RPB	Recognized Professional Body. Created by the Financial Services Act (1986) and monitored by the Securities and Investment Board.
RS232 and RS232C	The serial port needed to link computers in communications. It consists of a twenty-five-pin D-shaped connector.
RVC	Reverse Voice Channel.
Safe house	A secure area.

Safe room	A room shielded by sound- and vibration-absorbing material to prevent interference by radio signals or radiation. Popular in sensitive embassies.
Salami	A belligerent computer programme used in fraud. So named because of its object of slicing small sums of money from different accounts and transferring them to an account held by the fraudster.
Sam Spade	A colloquial term for a private investigator.
Sanitize	To render a place or an area free of all incriminating evidence. Also known as 'cleansing'.
SAS	The Special Air Service, which is made up of three squadrons, namely 2:1, 2:2 and 2:3. An élite Special Force highly trained in countering terrorist or subversive threats. Also known as the 'Regiment'.
SAT	Supervisory Audio Tone.
Scanner	A receiver which is able to scan a fixed part of the radio spectrum.
Scrambler	A device used to encode and then decode sensitive messages.
Screamer	A system used in counter-espionage to identify whether cables have been compromised. Identification is by means of a 'screaming' sound.
Secret Squirrels	The name given to BT engineers who assist in the use of Home Office-agreed telephone taps.
SEM	Single European Market
Series radio tap	A radio transmitter attached in series which obtains power from the telephone line to which it is attached.
SFA	Securities and Futures Authority, which arose from the merger of the AFBD and the TSA in April 1991. A self-regulatory organization.
SFO	Serious Fraud Office.
Shotgun mike	A specialized type of directional microphone used mainly outside and for picking up conversations from some distance away.
SIB	Securities and Investment Board, which oversees the UK self-regulated financial markets.

Simplex	A system of transmission in one direction only.
Six	MI6
Sleeper	A long-term agent whose services may not be required for years.
Smartcard	A credit-card-sized microprocessor used to store data.
Spectrum analyser	Equipment used in counter-measures to display a given frequency band.
Spike mike	A special microphone attached to a spike which is used to penetrate thick surfaces so as to create a better quality of reception.
Spook	An intelligence operative. Also known as a ghost.
Spurt	A form of very high-speed transmission to send sensitive messages. Also known as 'Burst'.
SRO	Self-Regulatory Organization.
Sting	An American term which is the same as a 'false-flag' in the UK – the use of a pretext to gain access to information or a place.
Stop loss	The term given to describe the level at which investment managers automatically decide to sell their stakeholdings.
Subbie	A sub-contractor. These people are common in the security industry where, for reasons of cost, discretion and accountability, the concept of the extended line, where as few people know each other as possible, is popular.
Surveillance	The art of discreet but constant monitoring by physical and electronic methods.
Sweep	A physical and electronic check for the presence of electronic eavesdropping devices.
Synchronous	The transmission of data where timing information is superimposed onto pure data.
Takeover code	The City of London Code of Takeovers and Mergers which is administered by the Stock Exchange but does not have the force of law.
Tap	An electronic eavesdrop which is often illegal.
Tasking	The use of delegation to achieve an objective. An aspect of command and

control with few of the component parts knowing the whole story.

Telephone analyzer
Used to carry out tests on telephones and switchboards to see if they have been compromised.

Tell-tale
The use of a trap to see whether an area has been infiltrated.

Tempest
A series of US standards prescribing limits for electromagnetic radiation from computer installations and peripherals. Also known as Van Eck 'Freaking' after Willem Van Eck, the Dutch scientist who discovered the phenomenon.

Third Market
An addition to the Unlisted Securities Market (USM) which started trading on 26 January 1987.

Third-wire bugs
Double-purpose bugs which act as standard telephone bugs but when the telephone is not in use use their internal microphone to bug the room which houses the telephone.

Tone generator
A device used to activate an infinite device. Occasionally known as a whistle or harmonica.

Trap-door
A technique of electronic crime popular with fraudsters whereby data quite literally falls through a 'trap-door' created by a computer virus.

Triangulation
The method used to locate a beacon by the use of multiple direction-finding receivers.

Triple Witching Hour
A quarterly phenomenon which occurs in Wall Street on the third Friday of the last month of the quarter when a whole variety of options are called at the same time, the sheer volume rendering the market very volatile.

Trojan Horse
A hidden piece of normally belligerent code which self-destructs as soon as its fraudulent mission has been fulfilled.

Trust
Property used for the benefit of another via the use of nominees or trustees. Popular with offshore entities where the concealment of assets is of paramount importance.

Tube mike
A small sealed box containing a microphone with a thin plastic tube

protruding from the box which enables the microphone to concentrate on sounds emanating from the direction in which the tube is pointing.

UHF
Ultra High Frequency. It is UHF which carries the pictures on a TV set, whilst the sound is carried by VHF.

UPSI
Unlisted Price Sensitive Information.

USM
Unlisted Security Market.

Utility programme
A PC Tools programme that enables one to retrieve deleted documents – not a software application per se but often used in 'software salvage'.

Van Eck Freaking
VDU-emitted electromagnetic radiation discovered by Dutch scientist Willem Van Eck. Also known as 'Tempest'.

Venture capital
The release of funds to new unquoted businesses to help them to start trading.

VHF
Very High Frequency. The medium by which sound waves are carried.

Virus
A destructive computer programme which can copy itself to and from computer disks, into systems and across entire computer networks.

VOX
A voice-activated system which conserves tape life and power supply.

VPK
The Military-Industrial Commission of the former USSR.

Walk-past
A form of reconnaissance used in surveillance, similar to a drive-past.

White noise
An unintelligible and nauseating noise which makes listening unpleasant. The product of successful jamming, it can be used as an aid to interrogation.

White knight
A player in a takeover battle who rescues the victim from the advances of the predator. Occasionally the victim will contact a 'white knight' whom he feels he would prefer to own the business.

Z score
A figure that uses a company's financial accounts to indicate the viability of a business.

APPENDIX 2

List of useful sources mentioned in the text

A–Z of Business Information
  Sources
Croner House
London Rd
Kingston-upon-Thames
Surrey KT2 6SR

Army & Navy Club
36 Pall Mall
London SW1

Army Records Office
Ministry of Defence Public
  Record Office
Bourne Avenue
Hayes
Middlesex UB3 1RF

Aslib Publications
20–24 Old Street
London EC1V 9AP

Bodleian Library
Oxford University
Broad Street
Oxford OX1 3BG

British Library
St Pancras (New Building)
London W1V 4BH

Cambridge University Library
West Rd
Cambridge CB3 9DR

Cavalry & Guards Club
127 Piccadilly
London W1

CCN Systems Ltd
Talbot House
Talbot St
Nottingham NG1 5HF

Chartered Association of
  Certified Accountants
29 Lincoln's Inn Fields
London WC2A 3EE

City Business Library
Brewers Hall Garden
London Wall
London EC1

Companies House
55–71 City Road
London EC1Y 1BB

Companies House
Crown Way
Maindy
Cardiff CF4 3UZ

CXT
1 Tanner St
London SE1 3LE

Debretts Peerage Ltd
73–77 Britannia Rd
London SW6 2JY

DTI
1–19 Victoria St
London SW1

Dun and Bradstreet
 International
Holmers Farm Way
High Wycombe
Bucks HP12 4UI

Durrant's Press Cuttings
103 Whitecross St
London EC1Y 8QT

DVLC
Swansea
SA99 1AA

Extel Financial Ltd
13 Epworth St
London EC2A 4DL

General Register Office
St Katherine's House
10 Kingsway
London WC2B 6JP

HMSO
15 Whitehall
London SW1A 2DD

IBCA Banking Analysis Ltd
2 Eldon House
Eldon St
London EC2

Infolink
Coombe Cross
2–4 South End
Croydon CR0 1DL

Institute of Actuaries
Staple Inn Hall
High Holborn
London WC1V 7QJ

Institute of Bankers
10 Lombard St
London EC3

Institute of Chartered
 Accountants
Moorgate Place
London EC2

Institute of Chartered
 Accountants of Scotland
24–30 Holborn
London EC1N 2JB

International Press Cuttings
 Bureau
224–36 Walworth Rd
London SE17 1JE

Jordan & Sons Ltd
Jordan House
Brunswick Place
London N1 6EE

Kelly's Business Directory
Windsor Court
East Grinstead House
East Grinstead
West Sussex

Kompass
Windsor Court
East Grinstead House
East Grinstead
West Sussex

Land Registry
32 Lincoln's Inn Fields
London WC2A 3PH

Lloyd's Register of Shipping
71 Fenchurch St
London EC3M 4BS

Loughborough University of
 Technology
Ashby Rd
Loughborough LE1 3TU

Ministry of Defence Library
Main Building
Whitehall
London SW1A 2HB

MW Douglas & Co. Ltd
Crown House
2 Crown Dale
London SE19 3NQ

National Library of Scotland
George IV Bridge
Edinburgh EH1 1EW

National Library of Wales
Aberystwyth
Dyfed SY23 3BU

Naval Records Office
Ministry of Defence Public
 Records Office
Bourne Avenue
Hayes
Middlesex UB3 1RF

Newsclip Ltd
St Marks Studio
Chillingworth Rd
London N7

Office of Receiverships and
 Bankruptcies
Commercial Union House
22 Martineau Square
Birmingham B2 4UP

Patents Office
Cardiff Rd
Newport
Gwent NP9 1RH

Patents Search and Advisory
 Service
Southampton Buildings
Chancery Lane
London WC2A 1AR

RAF Club
128 Piccadilly
London W1

RAF Records
RAF Innsworth
Gloucester GL3 1EZ

Romeike and Curice Ltd
Press Clippings
Burhale House
Green Lanes
London N13 5TP

Royal Courts of Justice
Strand
London WC2

Science Reference and
 Information Service
Southampton Buildings
Chancery Lane
London WC2

Standard Press Cuttings Ltd
40 Bowling Green Lane
London EC1R 0NE

Thomson Bank Directory
c/o Thomson Financial
 Publishing
P.O. Box 65
Scokie
Illinois 60076
USA

Trinity College Library
College Street
Dublin 2
Eire

APPENDIX 3

List of prominent database producers and their capabilities

DATABASE NAME	PRODUCER'S DETAILS	DETAILS OF INFORMATION PROVIDED
Kompass online	Reed Information Services Ltd Windsor Court East Grinstead House East Grinstead West Sussex RH19 1XA Tel: (0342) 326972	UK and European company details held. The UK files use details from Kompass, Kelly's, *The Directory of Directors, Dial Industry* and *British Export UK Trade Names.* 1.5 million UK companies are listed and additional information is held on 162,000 UK companies. Over 40 company characteristics can be searched and retrieved on this file. Regarding the European files, information is held on nearly 300,000 European companies and is taken from 11 European *Kompass* directories. This database can select companies by up to 110,000 industrial, product or service classifications and provides details of over 235,000 named executives with their job titles.
McCarthy Company Fact Sheets	McCarthy Information Ltd Manor House Ash Walk Warminster Wiltshire BA12 8PY	Information is held on c.1,000 UK companies and c.100 overseas companies quoted on the London Stock Exchange. Typical information available includes director's and company secretarial details, auditors, SEC code, five years' financial history, a description of the company's activities, head office address and telephone number and the companies capitalization.

		All records can be searched by turnover, profit, geographic location, activity or earnings/share. The system is good for assessing an individual's directorships.
Dun & Bradstreet's Key British Enterprises	Dun & Bradstreet Ltd Holmers Farm Way High Wycombe Buckinghamshire HP12 4UL Tel: (0494) 423680	Information held on the main 50,000 UK companies, including company name and address, telephone/fax/telex numbers, directors' addresses, details of chief executive and functions, annual sales, branch locations, numbers of employees, geographic markets, export sales, industry data and trade names, awards and warrants.
Dun's Marketing UK online	Dun & Bradstreet Ltd Holmers Farm Way High Wycombe Buckinghamshire HP12 4UL Tel: (0494) 423680	Includes records of company name, address, telephone/fax numbers, directors, employee total, sales turnover, import/export information, formation details and UK and US SIC codes and descriptions.
Jordan's	Jordan & Sons Ltd Jordan House Brunswick Place London N1 6EE Tel: (071) 253 3030	Information on over 2 million UK company records, including dissolved companies, showing date of incorporation, name of company, address of registered office, mortgages, charges, annual return, accounts, name changes and notice of recently filed documents.

DATABASE NAME	PRODUCER'S DETAILS	DETAILS OF INFORMATION PROVIDED
Who Owns Whom	Dun & Bradstreet Ltd Holmers Farm Way High Wycombe Buckinghamshire HP12 4UL Tel: (0494) 423680	This is similar in concept to a hard copy version of *Who's Who*. Information is held on over 21,000 international parent companies and over 300,000 subsidiaries. It is able to identify the group to which the company belongs or provide lists of companies with similar criteria. The system is a global company information source and, as well as providing the usual company information, it will also provide details of structured links within corporate groups.
Infolink	Infolink Ltd 2–4 South End Croydon CR0 1DL Tel: (081) 686 7777	Over 44 million records are held on individuals, with over 1 million records being held on UK companies and a further 1 million records being held on unlimited businesses. The system keeps details on all UK registered companies, including those which have been dissolved. Most information is provided instantaneously, though some enquiries on companies will have to wait for 24 or 48 hours for the information to be put online. Company information includes accounting ratios for the last three years of accounts.

Company Profile	Infocheck Ltd 28 Scrutton Street London EC2A 4RQ Tel: (071) 377 8872	Full details of company information on over 275,000 UK registered companies.
CCN Business Information	CCN Business Information Ltd Abbey House Abbeyfield Road Lenton Nottingham NG7 2SW Tel: (0602) 863864	Provides information on over 2 million UK registered companies, partnerships, sole traders and some overseas companies. Typical information includes credit information, details of county court judgements and bankruptcies, all mortgages and charges registered since 1984, accounting ratios and unsecured creditor information.
Dunsprint	Dun & Bradstreet Ltd Holmers Farm Way High Wycombe Buckinghamshire HP12 1UL Tel: (0494) 424444	A credit database covering 18 million companies in over 110 countries. The data is divided between 10 computer installations located in the UK, Germany, Australia, Hong Kong, Singapore, New Zealand, Japan, USA and Canada. The system provides three services, namely, Dun's Financial Profiles, Payment Analysis Reports and Business Information Reports.

DATABASE NAME	PRODUCER'S DETAILS	DETAILS OF INFORMATION PROVIDED
FT Mergers & Acquisitions	*Financial Times* Business Information Tower Hosue Southampton Sreet London WC2E 7HA Tel: (071) 240 9391	A mergers and acquisitions database covering mainly UK, US and European companies. The system contains c.10 million reports representing: completed deals, plans to acquire, agreed bids, plans to merge and management buy outs. Approximately one third of the file is dedicated to planned deals and the remaining two thirds is dedicated to completed deals.
UK Mergers & Acquisitions	Extel Financial Ltd Fitzroy House 13–17 Epworth Street London EC2A 4DL Tel: (071) 251 3333	The system tracks all transactions involving a UK target and includes overseas divestments by UK based companies. Over 200 data items are available for UK analysis. Information contains proactive details on companies seeking to acquire or be acquired, current and historic information on pending, finished, unconditional and unsuccessful deals, transaction techniques including stake purchases and repurchases and consensus forecasts and standard multiples on targets and acquirers. The system will also allow the user access to the USA's M&A database containing over 26,000 transactions.

ICC British Company Financial Datasheets	ICC Information Group Ltd 72 Oldfield Road Hampton Middlesex TW12 2HQ Tel: (081) 783 1122	For c.110,000 UK companies, the service provides financial information and company details including directors details, assets and liabilities, trading address, parent company, turnover and profit. For 90,000 companies, the service also has details on accounting ratios.
ICC Stockbroker Research	ICC Information Group Ltd 72 Oldfield Road Hampton Middlesex TW12 2HQ Tel: (081) 783 1122	Provides details from prominent UK & International stockbrokers of reports of comparisons, projections and evaluations of industry trends and individual company's performance. Information includes products and brand data, revenue evaluation, background, product development, medium term forecasts and 5–10 year financial summaries. Of all of the available reports, c.60 per cent cover UK companies, c.20 per cent cover European companies and the remaining 20 per cent cover companies from elsewhere in the world such as Japan, the Far East and Australia.
ICC Business Research	ICC Information Group Ltd Field House 72 Oldfield Road Hampton Middlesex TW12 2HQ Tel: (081) 783 1122	Provides details of market and industrial background, detailed financial information on companies and expert analytical reports.

DATABASE NAME	PRODUCER'S DETAILS	DETAILS OF INFORMATION PROVIDED
Datastream company accounts	Datastream International Ltd Monmouth House 56–64 City Road London EC1Y 2AL Tel: (071) 250 3000	Provides accounts and equity data in UK, Japanese, North American and West European Companies.
FIND – Financial Institutions Database	Tekron Publications Tekron House Small Business Industrial Estate Hall Lane Walton-on-the-Naze Essex CO14 8HT Tel: (0255) 677868	General information, including accounts, on UK financial institutions such as Building Societies, Insurance companies and Banks.
Exstat	Extel Financial Ltd Fitzroy House 13–17 Epworth Street London EC2A 4DL Tel: (071) 251 3333	Companies incorporated in UK, Japan, Australia and Continental Europe. Within the UK, the system covers Stock Exchange listed companies, USM companies and private companies identified in the Times 1000.

Jordan's	Jordan & Sons Ltd Jordan House Brunswick Place London N1 6EE Tel: (071) 253 3030	Information provided on companies via three files, namely: Jordan Watch, Jordan Survey and Jordan New Companies. Jordan Watch covers companies which satisfy one of three criteria, namely: a turnover in excess of £1 million, pre tax profits of £50,000 or shareholder funds of over £1 million. Where a company turnover is less than £1 million per annum then any available information will be covered by Jordan Survey.
Profile	FT Profile Information PO Box 12 Sunbury-on-Thames Middlesex TW16 7UD Tel: (0932) 761444	Extensive current and historic information on specific and general matters. A five main command structure to access information makes the system very user friendly. Contents include *The Times*, the *Sunday Times*, the *Telegraph*, the *Sunday Telegraph, Guardian, Today, Observer, Financial Times, Independent, Independent on Sunday, Scotsman, European, Banker, Jordan's, Extel, MSI Market Research, Campaign, New Scientist, McCarthy, Wall Street Journal, Dow Jones, Business Weekly, Washington Post* and the *Hoppenstedt* in both English and German.
Hermes	FT Profile Information As above.	Business news.

DATABASE NAME	PRODUCER'S DETAILS	DETAILS OF INFORMATION PROVIDED
FT Business Reports	FT Information online As above.	Business news.
McCarthy online	McCarthy Information Ltd Manor House Ash Walk Warminster Wiltshire BA12 8PY Tel: (0985) 215151	Business news.
Reuters Textline	Reuter Finsbury Data Reuters Ltd 85 Fleet Street London EC4P 4AJ Tel: (071) 250 1122	Business news.
Nexis	Mead Data Central International House 1 St Katherine's Way London E1 9UN Tel: (071) 488 9187	Business news.

Lexis		Database of legal cases.
Topic	The Stock Exchange Old Broad Street London EC2N 1HP Tel: (071) 588 2355	Automated stock exchange prices being updated each minute.
IMF International Financial Statistics	IMF – Bureaux of Statistics 700 19th Street NW Washington DC 20431, USA Tel: 202 473 7900	Financial and economic details.
Bank of England Databank	Bank of England Threadneedle Street London EC2R 8AH Tel: (071) 601 4918	Financial and economic information.
CSO Databank	Central Statistical Office Great George Street London SW1P 4AQ Tel: (071) 270 6386	Financial and economic information.

DATABASE NAME	PRODUCER'S DETAILS	DETAILS OF INFORMATION PROVIDED
Tradstadt	Data-star Plaza Suite 114 Jermyn Street London SW1Y 6HJ Tel: (071) 930 5503	Trade information.
MAID – Market Analysis & Info. Database	MAID Systems Ltd Maid House 26 Baker Street London W1M 1DF Tel: (071) 935 6460	Media and marketing information.
MEAL – Media Expenditure and Analysis	Media Expenditure and Analysis 63 St Martin's Lane London WC2 Tel: (071) 240 1903	Media and marketing information.
Business Periodicals Index	H W Wilson Company c/o Thomson Henry Ltd London Road Sunningdale Berkshire SL5 0EP Tel: (0990) 24615	Information on business management.

APPENDIX 4

List of additional useful information sources

NEWSLETTERS

Blackwells Osney Mead Oxford OX2 0EL Tel: (0865) 240201	Professional information services and scientific publications
Elsevier International 256 Banbury Road Oxford OX2 7DH Tel: (0865) 512242	Regular science-based bulletins.
FT Business Information Ltd Tower House Southampton Street London WC2E 7HA Tel: (071) 240 9391	Over 30 specialist titles covering 10 subject areas, namely: law, investments, finance, mergers and acquisitions, international markets, pharmaceuticals, media, fin-tech, energy and commodities.

FIRMS OF STOCKBROKERS PROVIDING REPORTS AND ANALYSES

NAME OF REPORT	PRODUCER'S DETAILS	DESCRIPTION OF REPORT/ANALYSIS
UK Economic Analysis	Goldman Sachs 5 Old Bailey London EC4M 7AH Tel: (071) 248 6464	A bi-monthly publication which provides details on market movements.
Economic Forecasts	UBS-Philips & Drew 120 Moorgate London EC2M 6XP Tel: (071) 628 4444	A monthly publication which analyses changes in markets. Supplemented weekly.
Economic Outlook	Hoare Govett Ltd 4 Broadgate London EC2M 7LE Tel: (071) 601 0101	A report which analyses the economy and is produced four to six times each year.
UK Economic Assessment	James Capel & Co James Capel House 6 Bevis Marks London EC3A 7JQ Tel: (071) 621 0011	A quarterly produced assessment of the economy which is supplemented by Monthly Economic Signals.

ECONOMIC TRENDS AND FORECASTING

NAME OF REPORT	PRODUCER'S DETAILS	DESCRIPTION OF FORECAST
Economic Review	City University Business School Frobisher Crescent Barbican Centre London EC2Y 8HB Tel: (071) 920 0111	An economic forecast which is supported by the Economic Science and Research Centre (ESRC) and which is produced four times per year.
Economic Outlook	London Business School Centre for Economic Forecasting Sussex Place Regent's Park London NW1 4SA Tel: (071) 262 5050	An ESRC-supported economic forecast which is produced thrice yearly and supplemented during the rest of the year.
CBI Economic Situation Report	CBI Economic Trends Department Confederation of British Industry Centre Point 103 New Oxford Street London WC1A 1DU Tel: (071) 379 7400	An independent forecasting service which produces economic reports each month.

Country Report	The Economist Intelligence Unit 40 Duke Street London W1A 1DW Tel: (071) 493 6711	Produced quarterly, with business updates provided on a monthly basis. The EIU also provides an International Economic Appraisal Service and a Business Information Forecasting Service.
Business Opinion Survey	The Institute of Directors Policy Unit 116 Pall Mall London SW1Y 5ED Tel: (071) 839 1233	Produced six times each year.
Various guides	The Henley Centre 2 Tudor Street Blackfriars London EC4Y 0AA Tel: (071) 353 9961	The Henley Centre produces a variety of economic forecasts and guides on various subjects throughout the year. For example: (a) Framework Forecasts for the UK Economy – monthly. (b) Leisure Futures – quarterly. (c) Directors guide – monthly. (d) Framework Forecasts for the EC economies – monthly.

DIRECTORIES

NAME	PRODUCER'S DETAILS	BRIEF SUMMARY OF SCOPE
Advertiser's Annual	Reed Information Services Windsor Court East Grinstead House East Grinstead West Sussex RH19 1XB	The annual comprises three volumes and is colour coded. Volume 1 covers advertising agencies and PR companies. Volume 2 extends into the global media market and includes details of papers, magazines, TV, radio and poster companies. Volume 3 deals with suppliers and services.
The City Directory	Woodhead-Faulkner (Publishers) Ltd 8 Market Passage Cambridge CB2 3PF	Provides extensive information on leading figures in the City of London.
Crawford's Directory of City Connections	The Economist Newspapers Ltd 25 St James' Street London SW1A 1HG	Demonstrates the inter-linking of prominent financial institutions and the main professional advisors of Stock Exchange listed companies.
Becket's Directory of the City of London	Becket Publications Ltd 4 St John's Place London EC1M 4AH	Covers over 550 institutions and over 3,000 individuals with c. 1,500 detailed biographies.

Directory of Directors	Reed Information Services (As above)	A two-volume work providing details of over 60,000 directors of c. 16,500 prominent UK companies.
UK Analysts Who's Who	Citygate Communications Ltd 7 Birchin Lane London EC3V 9BY	Provides details of over 1,200 analysts in over 60 companies, including some with photographs.
Who's Who in Scotland	Carrick Publishing 28 Miller Road Ayr KA7 2AY	Basic biographical information on over 5,000 individuals
Who Owns Whom: UK & Eire	Dun & Bradstreet Ltd Holmers Farm Way High Wycombe Bucks. HP12 4UL	Details on over 6,500 companies including parents, subsidiaries and associated companies.
Who's Who in the City	Macmillan Press Ltd 4 Little Essex Street London WC2R 3LF	Provides biographical details on over 8,00 major figures working in the UK financial service industry.

NAME	PRODUCER'S DETAILS	BRIEF SUMMARY OF SCOPE
Major Companies of Western Europe	Graham & Trotmann Ltd Sterling House 66 Wilton Road London SW1V 1DE	A three-volume publication covering 7,000 companies of which 2,000 are UK companies. Companies are listed according to their country of origin and details include directors, senior executives, bankers, subsidiaries, trade names and financial details.
Hambro Company Guide	Hemmington Scott Publishing Ltd 6–7 City Innovation Centre 26–31 Whiskin Street London EC1R 0BP	Produced quarterly and provides details on UK companies, including some Business Expansion Scheme companies.
The Times 1000	Times Books Ltd 16 Golden Square London W1R 4BN	The 1,000 leading companies in the UK and overseas. Details include principle accounts, managing director, chairman, capital employed, net profit, numbers of employees, turnover, exports and market capitalization.
UK's 10,000 Largest Companies	ELC International Sinclair House The Avenue London W13 8BR	Basic company information including name, address, telephone number, sales details, number of employees, assets, industrial sector and capital structure.

CD-ROM INFORMATION SERVICES

NAME OF SYSTEM	PRODUCER'S DETAILS	BRIEF SUMMARY OF SCOPE
FAME – Financial Analysis Made Easy	Jordan & Sons Ltd Jordan House Brunswick Place London N1 6EE Tel: (071) 253 3030	Provides detailed financial information on over 75,000 UK registered companies, including addresses, key duties, numbers of employees, holding companies, subsidiaries and main directors.
Kompass CD	Reed Information Services Ltd East Grinstead House East Grinstead West Sussex RH19 1XA	Information held on over 150,000 UK registered companies.

APPENDIX 5

List of statutes found in the text

Births and Deaths Registration Act (1926)
Computer Misuse Act (1990)
Computer Virus Eradication Act (USA) (1989)
Control of Pollution Act (1974)
Criminal Damage Act (1971)
Data Protection Act (1984)
Design, Patents and Copyright Act (1988)
Electronic Communications Privacy Act (USA) (1986)
Freedom of Information Act (USA) (1966)
Interception of Communications Act (1985)
Population (Statistics) Acts (1938) and (1960)
Rehabilitation of Offenders Act (1974)
Representation of the People Act (1983)
Theft Act (1968)
Theft Act (1978)
Trade Mark Act (1937)
Wireless Telegraphy Act (1949)

NOTES AND SOURCES

CHAPTER 1

1 Letter to Japanese Communist Party chairman Saneo Nozaka, June 1962, quoted in John Barron, *KGB – The Secret Work of Soviet Secret Agents*, Hodder & Stoughton, 1974.
2 Numbers XIII, quoted in Christopher Andrew, *Secret Service*, Hodder & Stoughton, 1985.
3 Joshua II, quoted in Andrew, op. cit.
4 Phillip Knightley, *The Second Oldest Profession: The Spy as Bureaucrat, Patriot, Fanaticist and Whore*, André Deutsch, 1986.
5 Andrew, op. cit.
6 Knightley, op. cit.
7 Ladislas Farrago, *The Game of the Foxes*, Hodder & Stoughton, 1972; referred to also in Knightley, op. cit.
8 Thomas H. Etzold, 'The (F)utility Factor: German Information Gathering in the US 1933–41', in *Military Affairs*, Vol. 39, No. 2, 1975.
9 John Barron, *KGB: The Secret Work of Soviet Secret Agents*, Hodder & Stoughton, 1974.
10 John Barron, op. cit.
11 Hillsman, *On Intelligence*, quoted in Knightley, op. cit.
12 Harry Rositzke, *America's Secret Operations*, quoted in Knightley, op. cit.

CHAPTER 2

1 St Matthew VII.
2 Frederick Forsyth, *The Day of the Jackal*, Hutchinson, 1979.
3 Noel Coward, 'Operette'.

CHAPTER 3

1 Oscar Wilde, *The Importance of Being Earnest*, Act 1, 1895.
2 Sir Arthur Conan-Doyle, 'The Hound of the Baskervilles', in *The Long Stories of Sherlock Holmes*, John Murray, 1954.

3 Quoted in Hugo Cornwall, *The Industrial Espionage Handbook*, Random Century, 1991.
4 *Los Angeles Times*, 19 March 1991; Wendy Zellner and Bruce Hager, 'Corporate spying. Dumpster raids? That's not very ladylike, Avon – Mary Kay is seeing hot pink over its rivals' espionage tactics', *Business Week*.
5 *Sunday Times Magazine*, 7 October 1990.
6 *Sunday Times*, 17 November 1991.
7 Article by Peter Heims in *Professional Security*, No. 7, January/ February 1992.
8 Ibid.
9 *Guardian*, December 1992.
10 Quoted in Chapman Pincher, *Traitors – the Labyrinths of Treason*, Sidgwick & Jackson, 1987, Ch. 3.
11 Ibid.
12 Kim Philby, *Sunday Times*, 17 December 1967.

CHAPTER 4

1 William Shakespeare, 'The Rape of Lucrece'.
2 *Guardian*, 26 June 1991; *Today*, 26 June 1990, 8 April 1991; *The Times*, 18 June 1990, 1 and 6 May 1991; *Daily Telegraph*, 1 May 1991; *Sunday Times*, 17 and 24 June, 5 August 1990, 7 April and 5 May 1991, 24 January 1993; *Evening Standard*, 12 March 1993.
3 *Forbes* magazine, October 1991.
4 'Britain's richest 300', *Sunday Times Magazine*, 10 May 1992; 'Britain's richest 400', *Sunday Times Magazine*, 4 April 1993.
5 Mark Skipworth and Greg Hadfield, 'NatWest loophole leaks customer secrets', *Sunday Times*, 21 March 1993.
6 C. Griffiths in *International Criminal Police Review*, No. 377, quoted in Cornwall, op. cit.

CHAPTER 5

1 Democritus, quoted in Brian Freemantle, *The Steal – Counterfeiting and Industrial Espionage*, Michael Joseph, 1986, Ch. 17.

CHAPTER 6

1 William Shakespeare, *Hamlet*, Act IV, scene v.
2 Colonel General Mikhailov, Head of the Soviet GRU, quoted in 'Industrial Spying – the Russian Threat against British Industry', *Professional Security*, No. 9, May 1992, p. 31.
3 Leonard M. Fuld, *Competitor Intelligence*, John Wiley & Sons, 1985; Cornwall, op. cit.
4 Quoted in Norman Bottom and Robert J. Gallati, *Industrial Espionage: Intelligence Techniques and Counter Measures*, Butterworths, 1984, cited in Cornwall, op. cit.
5 Cornwall, op. cit.
6 *Fortune* magazine, 7 November 1988.

CHAPTER 7

1 Malcolm Muggeridge, *Chronicles of Wasted Time*, Vol. II, Collins, 1973.
2 Nick Kochan and Bob Whittington, *Bankrupt – the BCCI Fraud*, Gollancz,1991.

CHAPTER 8

1 William Shakespeare, *Macbeth*, (act and scene no.?)
2 'Documents from the US Espionage Den', *Independent on Sunday*, 30 September 1990.

CHAPTER 9

1 Dante, *The Divine Comedy*.
2 *The Times*, 13 February 1988.
3 *Guardian*, 14 June and 16 July 1991.
4 'Calcutt – Curse or Cure?', *Sunday Times*, 17 January 1993.
5 Quoted in John Wingfield, *Bugging – a Complete Survey of Electronic Surveillance Today*, Robert Hale, 1984.
6 Ibid.
7 Ibid.
8 Article on tracking reindeers in Canada using the 'Doppler shift' system and satellite tracking, *Economist*, 27 November 1993.
9 *Hansard*, May 1989.
10 *Sunday Times*, 11 November 1990; Cornwall, op. cit.

11 Belden Menkus, 'Cellular telephone use can be dangerous – auto safety and the exposure of confidential and sensitive business information', *Modern Office Technology*, Vol. 35, p. 66, August 1990.

12 'Cellular Radio: Vulnerability to Attack', (source and date unavailable).

13 'Cellular Radio', op. cit.

CHAPTER 10

1 The Second Epistle General of Peter, I.19.

2 John Wingfield, *Bugging – A Complete Survey of Electronic Surveillance Today*, Robert Hale, 1984.

3 Ibid.

4 Ibid.

5 Quoted in Christian Brann, *Pass the Port Again*, Oxfam, 1984.

CHAPTER 11

1 Steve Gold in the newsletter *Computer Security*, quoted in *Hugo Cornwall's New Hacker's Handbook*, Century Hutchinson, 1989.

2 Ibid.

3 Steve Gold, *Hugo Cornwall's New Hacker's Handbook*, op. cit.; Brian Dumaine, 'Corporate Spies Snoop to Conquer', *Fortune* magazine, 7 November 1988.

4 Quoted in 'Tap-proof data communications', *Defence, Communications and Security Review 1990*, Diplomatic and Consular Year Book International Ltd.

5 Quoted in Steve Gold, *Hugo Cornwall's New Hacker's Handbook*, op. cit.

CHAPTER 12

1 John Philpot Curran, 'Upon the Right of Election of the Lord Mayor of Dublin', speech, 10 July 1790.

2 Quoted in Peter Thompsett, 'Computer Security – Redial Computer Access Control', *Defence, Communications and Security Review 1990*, Diplomatic and Consular Year Book International Ltd.

3 Quoted in Paul Abrahams, 'Hey-day for the hackers', *Financial Times*, 22 November 1988.

CHAPTER 13

1 Alfred, Lord Tennyson, 'Locksley Hall'.
2 J. M. Eder, *History of Photography*, 1945, p. 390, provided by Michael Pritchard, photographic historian, Christie's.
3 Morris Moses, *Spy Camera – the Minox Story*, Hove Foto Books, 1990.
4 Ibid.
5 Samuel Johnson, 'Vanity of Human Wishes', 1749.
6 *The Geographical Magazine*, May 1992.
7 Ibid, March 1991.
8 William S. Burroughs, *Deep Black*, Random House, New York, 1986; Cornwall op. cit.
9 Anne Hawkins, 'The Use of Remote Sensing to Control Area Aid Applications for Set Aside and Oilseeds in 1992', EC (EAGGF).

CHAPTER 14

1 William Shakespeare, *Othello*, Act III, Scene iii.
2 Freemantle, op. cit.
3 Ibid.
4 Author unknown. 'French Spy', *Security Management*, No. 35, November 1991, p. 10.
5 Patrice Duggan and Gale Eisenstadt, 'The new face of Japanese espionage', *Forbes* magazine, 12 November 1991.
6 Michael J. Stedman and Justin Martin, 'Still a distant second', *Across the Board*, November 1991.
7 Jan P. Herring, 'Business intelligence in Japan and Sweden: lessons for the US', *Journal of Business Strategy*, March/April 1992.
8 Duggan and Eisenstadt, op. cit.
9 Stephen Barlas, 'Does the CIA have a role in foreign market research?' *Marketing News*, Vol. 25, p. 2, 7 January 1991.
10 Michael J. Stedman, 'Can the government help?', *Across the Board*, November 1991.
11 John S. McClenahen, 'A job for the CIA? Should the Agency focus its expertise on industries overseas', *Industry Week*, 4 May 1992.
12 Amy Borrus, Rose Brady, Charles Hoots, Roger Schreffer, 'Government intelligence – should the CIA start spying for corporate America?', *Business Week*, 14 October 1991.

13 Amy Borrus,'Why pinstripes do not suit the cloak and dagger crowd (CIA spying on behalf of corporate America', *Business Week*, 17 May 1993.

14 Sumantra Ghoshal and Eleanour D. Westney, 'Organizing competitor analysis systems', *Strategic Management Journal*, Vol. 12, pp. 17–31, January 1991.

15 Leonard M. Fuld, 'Achieving total quality – Corning's competitive intelligence system', *Long Range Planning*, February 1992. Also Gary B. Roush, 'A program for sharing corporate intelligence' (Corning), *Journal of Business Strategy*, Vol. 12, pp. 4–7, January/February 1991.

16 Brian Dumaine, 'Corporate spies snoop to conquer', *Fortune* magazine, 7 November 1988.

CHAPTER 15

1 Percy Bysshe Shelley, 'Song to the Men of England'.

2 Quoted in Nicholas van der Bijl, 'The Soviet Threat – Industrial Spying', *Professional Security*, No. 9, May 1992.

3 Ibid.

The author and publishers have made every effort to trace and acknowledge sources, but will be happy to rectify any omissions in future editions.

INDEX